Secrets of Cistercian Music in Ireland
1142 - 1541

Cistercian abbey Churches
where the very stones
sing the psalms

Geraldine Carville

Acknowledgements

I wish to express my thanks to the following who have allowed me to reproduce plans: the Bibliothéque Nationale, Paris for Villard de Honnecourt's drawing of a Cistercian church; Wolfgang Mann Verlag GMBH Tietzenweg 75W-1000 Berlin 45, for Hano Hahn's diagram; the Black Friars Library, Vienna and HMML: PR No.8939; Hill Monastic Library USA for Letter 545 Codex 291 and Letter 546 Codex 291; Könemann Verlags gesellschaft mbH Bonner Strt. 126, D-50968 Koln for the 55 Vitruvian jars in the church of Loc-Dieu, Camille de Montalwet 1997; Dijon, Bibliotheque municipale.

The British Library MS 36929, microfilm and digital image 1-5823-02 MS 36929 folio 59 and photographs 155319 Add 36929 (1); 155322 Add 36929 11b^V; 155324 Add 36929 12^V; 155323 Add 36929 110^V; 155325 Add 36929 2^V; 155326 Add 36929 1^V; 155321 Add 36929 175^V. 59 Royal 2AXX f.17, Add 36881 f.2 map 'The grange of Outre-aube' Dom Milley (1708) and Viollet-le-Duc, from the map drawn by JR Leroux, L'Abbey de Clairvaux La Vie en Champagne 1986. The music of the Cistercian Abbey Assaroe, Our Lady of Bethlehem Abbey, Portglenone, Co. Antrim, Northern Ireland. DR David Howlett, Oxford for the Polyphonic Colophon to Cormac's Psalter.

To Dom Kevin and the community of Mount St. Joseph Abbey, Roscrea for permission to take photographs in the Abbey Church when my publisher Michael McKernon and I visited the Abbey in March 2006, I express my sincere thanks.

I would like to thank Dom Bede and Dom Joseph, formerly monk of Mount St. Bernard, England (now Abbot of N.D. du Calvaire, Canada) and Fr. Hilary, Fr. Gregory and Fr. Paul of that community; Dom Bernard and Fr. Alphonsus of Mellifont Abbey, Co. Louth; Bro. Finbar, Cantor, Fr. Martin and Dom Aengus, of Our Lady of Bethlehem Abbey, Co. Antrim; Fr. Richard, Dom Laurence, Fr. Ciaran and Fr. Nivard, Mount St. Joseph Abbey, Roscrea, Co. Tipperary for their invitations to speak to their communities and Dom Peter and the community of Our Lady of Bolton Abbey, Moone, Co. Kildare.

I would also like to thank Dr. M. Parkes, Geological Survey, Dublin; Rev. Prof. Martin McNamara, Dublin; Jack McLaren, B. Mus., Belfast; My sister in law Dr. Maeveen Carville, Queens University, Belfast; Dr. A. Refsum, Belfast; John Gray, Linenhall Library, Belfast; James Davis, Media Services, Queen's University Belfast; Caroline Poulain and Alexander Bakker, Dijon; Michael McKernon, Shanway Publications, Belfast; and my late parents, who gave my late brother Brendan and myself a love of learning and a love of music.

First Published in 2006 by Shanway Press, Belfast

ISBN 0-9543906-2-8   978-0-9543906-2-4

Published by Shanway Press, Belfast 2006
Design, Shanway, Belfast
Cover Design Michael McKernon

Dedicated to
Aisling
in memory of Brendan
and my parents
31st December 2005

'Vasa Cistercii,
Prócaí cré,
Macallaí na Bé
Ag Móradh Dé,
Secreta comsecrata.

Fr Ciaran Mt. St. Joseph Abbey, Roscrea

Solus qui cantat audit
'Only he who sings hears
1st Sermon, Song of Songs' – St Bernard

Fr. Martin, Bolton Abbey, Moone

Contents

Maps			vii
Plans and Illustrations			viii
Photographs			ix
Foreword			x
Preface			xi
Introduction			xii - xiii
Chapter	1.	Medieval Cistercian monasteries in Ireland	1
Chapter	2.	The Cistercian Order and Bernard (St.)	3
Chapter	3.	Clairvaux founds Irish houses, French monks arrive in Ireland	7
Chapter	4.	Cistercian Architecture and St. Agustine. The plan for Mellifont Abbey brought by the French monk Robert from Clairvaux Abbey	19
Chapter	5.	Monastic chant and acoustic jars	29
Chapter	6.	The Cistercians and music	41
Chapter	7.	Cantor, Sub-Cantor and Assistant Cantors	45
Chapter	8.	Psalter MS36929	51
Chapter	9.	The Scriptorium and Palaeography Manuscript 36929	59
Chapter	10.	The contents of Manuscript 36929	63
Chapter	11.	Theoretical and practical	79
Conclusion			85
Appendix 1			86
Appendix 2			87
Index			93
References			97
Bibliography			100

Maps

Map 1 - *Citeaux, routes via Dijon to Citeaux*   *3*

Map 2 - *The Diocesan Boundary change made by
         Saint Malachy for Mellifont Abbey, Co. Louth*   *8*

Map 3 - *The Charter Lands of Mellifont Abbey in Co. Louth*   *8*

Map 4 - *Site change of St. Bernard's Monastery from Clairvaux I to Clairvaux II*   *9*

Map 5 - *Monastic sites on the right bank of the River Nile*   *10*

Map 6 - *The Grange of Outre-Aube*   *18*

Map 7 - *Distribution of Acoustic Jars in Buildings in Medieval Europe*   *38*

Plans

Plan 1 - *Architectural Design - Villard de Honnecourt*   22

Plan 2 - *Bernard's (St) desire was that the ratio of the chords in music would give perfect symmetry and harmony to Cistercian Abbey Churches*   23

Plan 3 - *Ideal Cistercian Monastery (as presented by Aubert and Dimier)*   25

Plan 4 - *Design according to Braun*   26

Plan 5 - *Pole Design - Plan according to Hanno Hahn*   27

Plan 6 - *Plan of the Tower of Dunbrody Abbey*   32

Plan 7 - *The fifty five Vetruvian Jars in the Church of Loc-Dieu*   39

Illustrations

Illustration 1 - *Letter 'A' from the bible commissioned by St. Stephen Harding*   2

Illustration 1a - *ms13f. 150v (Colophon de la Bible). "that those reading it should not make any corrections into the text nor to erase any of those that have been entered"*   6

Illustration 2 - *Pots or Jars Detail*   30

Illustration 3 - *Section through a Greek theatre (after Bagenal and Wood)*   35

Illustration 4 - *Three rows of seats with thirteen cubicles for sounding vessels in each*   36

Illustration 5 - *A Roman theatre according to Vetruvius (after Landels 1967)*   37

Illustration 6 - *Cantor's Tablets*   46

Illustration 7 - *Polyphony Manuscript 36929*   52

Illustration 8 - *Four styles of word setting and plainsong (after Sturman P)*   54

Illustration 9 - *St Martial Manuscript Lux descendit*   55

Illustration 10 - *The system of Hexachords - and Guidonian Hand*   56, 57

Illustration 11 - *Folios 65v and 67v from the Ordinal of Rosglas*   61

Illustration 12 - *Psalm 15*   62

Illustration 13 - *Uses of the Psalms*   65

Illustration 14 - *Psalm 3 and Psalm 4*   68

Illustration 15 - *Psalm 1*   69

Illustration 16 - *Psalm 91*   70

Illustration 17 - *The Piper the Ordinal of Rosglas*   70

Illustration 18 - *Psalm 100*   71

Illustration 19 - *Psalm 150*   71

Illustration 20 - *Notes of equal value*   73

Illustration 21 - *The music of Abbey Assaroe, Co Donegal*   76, 77

Illustration 22 - *Royal 2.A.XX.f.17*   78

Illustration 23a - *Music from Manuscript 36929*   79, 82

Illustration 23b - *Is the same music in Gregorian Chant*   82

Illustration 23c - *Music transposed into modern staff notation*   83

Illustration 23d - *Music in modern staff notation with time signature and key signature*   84

Photographs

Photograph 1&2 - *Photo of a conduit, Mellifont Abbey*   10

Photograph 3 - *The Lavabo, Mellifont Abbey*   11

Photograph 4 - *Rock outcrops, Mellifont Abbey*   11

Photograph 5 - *The Mattock River at Mellifont Abbey*   13

Photograph 6 - *On the Grange of Outre-Aube, Clairvaux*   18

Photograph 7 - *Holy Cross Abbey*   19

Photograph 8 - *Window, Holy Cross Abbey*   22

Photograph 9 - *Carved stones, Baltinglass Abbey*   28

Photograph 10 - *Acoustic apertures in the tower of Dunbrody*   32

Photograph 11 - *The roof of the crossing, Dunbrody Abbey.*   33

Photograph 12 - *Acoustic apertures in the jambs of the walls of the windows in Dunbrody*   33

Photograph 13 - *Acoustic apertures in the tower of Dunbrody*   34

Photograph 14 - *Acoustic jar, Fountain Abbey, England*   35

Photograph 15 - *Father Richard, Cantor Mount St Joseph Abbey, Roscrea*   41

Photograph 16 - *Psalms and Canticles*   44

Photograph 17 - *Choir practice*   44

Photograph 18 - *Vespers, Mount St. Joseph Abbey*   45

Photograph 19 - *In the cloister*   47

Photograph 20 - *The Gothic method of vaulting gave a high light-filled sanctuary.*   48

Photograph 21 - *Salve Regina*   50

Photograph 22 - *Psalterium Davidicum, M. DCCC. LV.*   51

Photograph 23 -   *Studying the psalms*   53

Photograph 24 - *Boyle Abbey Co. Roscommon*   57

Photograph 25 - *Jerpoint Abbey, Co. Kilkenny*   58

Photograph 26 - *Carved stones from the ruins of Abbey Assaroe built into the graveyard wall*   77

When we consider the amount of scholarly research into Cistercian origins and life in the Middle Ages it is surprising that so little has been written about the monks' use of music and their understanding of it.

Dr Geraldine Carville, to whom the Cistercian Order already owes so much for her writings on Cistercian history, notably for her magisterial work on the Impact of the Cistercians on the Landscape of Ireland, has now put us and all who are interested in the history of the medieval period, further into her debt.

We now know that the first monks to live in Mellifont Abbey (the first Cistercian foundation in Ireland in 1142, made by St. Bernard at the behest of St. Malachy of Armagh) were French. Two letters from St. Bernard to the latter are reproduced which show their introduction to Ireland.

The monks had to sing the Divine Office seven times a day, and following the rule of St. Benedict they had to sing the entire Psalter each week. Dr Carville wondered for years just how the monks sang the Office, and what were the ratios between the architectural proportions of the Churches and the tonal scales used by the monks.

Dr Carville also became aware that there were indications in some of the medieval manuscripts for three part harmony in the singing, and she took the trouble to have these passages sung and recorded. She concludes that the Cistercian contribution to music in medieval Ireland was as she puts it "enormous and indeed comparable to their impact on the landscape!" For anyone interested in either medieval monastic life in Ireland or medieval music in monasteries or indeed in the contribution the Cistercian monks made to Irish culture this is the book to read. A remarkable production!

Fr. Nivard Kinsella OCSO STD, Mount St. Joseph Abbey, Roscrea

Preface

Pope Gregory the Great went to great trouble to have suitable chants arranged for the Divine Office and to have them sung by trained monks. The music became known as plain chant or plain song or Gregorian Chant. It was sung without harmonies, hence it was called plain. There was no known method of writing it down in those days and it had to be memorised.

This was the chant used by the Cistercians in Medieval Ireland (1142 - 1541). I was delighted to find references to music in two thirteenth century manuscripts, transcribed by Cistercian monks in Ireland, a Psalter manuscript 36929, British Library and manuscript C.32, Rawlinson Oxford, which would have been sung in the monastic church of the first foundation, Mellifont Abbey and other foundations that followed.

The plan of the Abbey Church for the Order of Citeaux was brought from France by the French monk, Robert for Mellifont Abbey. This I discovered shows how St Bernard's desire that the ratio of chords in music should be reflected in the layout of the Abbey church so that there is perfect symmetry or harmony in the architectural plan.

The Ordinal of Rosglas shows that the Cistercians in the Medieval period had knowledge of the hexachord which meant that they had a method of sight singing, they did not have to memorize the chant; manuscript 36929 shows that they had a knowledge of polyphony.

I feel that it is very important to see the monasteries in their immediate environment, their geographical location, geology, architecture, hydrology the political situation and the solitude of the monasteries, but it is most essential to understand the function of the monastic church and its raison d'etre, the worship of God in the chanting of the Divine Office. That is what I have endeavoured to do in this book, *Secrets of Cistercian Music in Ireland 1142 - 1541 Cistercian Abbey Churches where the very stones sing the psalms.*

Introduction

As far as can be ascertained, no study of Cistercian music, or the chanting of the Divine Office in medieval Ireland has been undertaken, yet for almost four hundred years and for twenty five percent of the daily life of the monks that is what took place in the abbey churches.

We are very fortunate to know that the plan for Mellifont Abbey, County Louth (1142), their first foundation, was brought by Robert from St. Bernard's monastery of Clairvaux, also to have two letters from St. Bernard, one to St. Malachy and one to Dermot McMurrough, which show that the first monks to reside in Mellifont Abbey and Baltinglass Abbey were French.

It was the required practice that each monastery had to provide books for the Divine Office for a daughter house and for Mellifont Abbey, these would have been brought from Clairvaux. In 1135, the General Chapter decided that the Gradual and the Antiphonary used by the Cistercians should be corrected, and commissioned St. Bernard of Clairvaux, their greatest authority on plain chant, to correct the manuscripts where necessary. Unfortunately St. Bernard was too busy trying to halt the Anacletus schism and the work had to be given to a monk called Guido. Recommendations regarding changes in the text were made to the General Chapter by the Commission. The alterations actually made are indicated and justified in a long passage commonly ascribed to St. Bernard but as Guido did the work, it is probable that he wrote the preface. The only part of the book that can be ascribed to St. Bernard with certainty is a short letter prefixed to the work, ordering in the name of the General Chapter its exclusive use as the text and music in all Cistercian houses. Later, with the increasing number of monks, copies were made in the scriptorium of each abbey for them. Manuscript 36929, Psalter of Cormac was produced in one of the thirty three medieval Cistercian abbeys in Ireland, but which one is not known. Could it have been Holy Cross Abbey, County Tipperary as the medieval poem says, it *was a house full of books and light and music of psalms*?

In researching this book, many questions had to be explored. Elsewhere when considering the geology of the site of Mellifont Abbey, I realised that it was an abbey in a quarry and to walk along the exterior perimeter of the east end is impossible. Then there was the requirement for square ended choirs, rather than the more elaborate chevet.

Many scholars have commented on the lack of decoration in medieval Cistercian churches and how they all follow a standard plan in layout. To measure the ruins of Cistercian abbey churches and express the results in numbers of feet and inches, or metres and centimetres, by those undertaking such work, and to achieve agreement is impossible. These would have to be taken in the foundation trenches, but where exactly, interior, exterior or central line? Furthermore, displacement in depth may have taken place such as might occur from earth tremors, subsidence or flooding.

Chanting the Divine Office was undertaken seven times each day as the aim was to sing the one hundred and fifty psalms in a week. The responsibility for this was the work of the Cantor, Sub-Cantor and Assistant Cantors but what did they do and how did they do it, was another question.

Otto von Simson, in his splendid book *The Gothic Cathedral* has mentioned structural ratios and proportions in medieval buildings, but how I wanted to know did these ratios contribute to harmony, what was their appeal? In February 2003, I made a 'breakthrough' when I realised that the modular layout as shown in the plan of the Cistercian architect Villard de Honnecourt's 'Church for the Order of Citeaux' could be related to the tonal scale.

On one occasion, when I was giving a talk to the Cistercian community of Mount St. Bernard, Leicestershire, England, I mentioned an acoustic tower in Ireland. The following day accompanied by Fr. Hilary and Fr. Paul of that community I visited Fountains Abbey and was delighted to see in the museum an acoustic jar of the type used in the Middle Ages. For me this was sound, something to be studied.

Following a talk I gave in May 2005, at the Cistercian Institute Conference, Western Michigan University, Kalamazoo, the reporter for *Cistercian Studies*, Fr. Charles Cummings, Holy Trinity monastery said *"the plain chant has indications for three part harmony, which we heard sung. The ratio of chords is reflected in the layout of the abbey church, so that there is perfect symmetry or harmony in the architectural plan. In the church walls are small openings for acoustic jars, used to reduce or amplify the sound, within the compass of two octaves. St. Augustine's teaching on music may have guided the Cistercians. St. Bernard insisted on hearing the word of God with clarity."*

I thank Fr. Charles Cummings for his outline report, as that is what this book is about. Perhaps it will lead to further research in Irish medieval Cistercian chant.

Today the excellence of the chanting of the same Divine Office by Cistercian monks has something in its modulated rhythm that stirs the very hearts of people, ever keenly alive to the influences of music which produces the happiest devotional results as the 'Pure Gregorian' never fails to do when rendered by the well-trained voices of men whose souls are in their work. This led me to study the attention given by them to music and to chanting the Divine Office, the same chant that was sung in Cistercian monasteries in Medieval Europe.

Chapter 1 | Medieval Cistercian Monasteries in Ireland

Right Rev. Dom Bernard Boyle, Mellifont Abbey, said to me "I want to know what they were doing in the monasteries in Ireland in the Middle Ages". This led me to search for Medieval Irish Cistercian manuscripts. In the first I obtained, were Letters 545 and 546, Codex 291 Vienna, which I published, then I found *Liber Sancti Marie de Valle Sancti Salvatoris,* which I edited, a facsimile of which was produced for the 800th anniversary of the Cistercian Abbey, Graiguenamanagh, County Kilkenny.

Manuscript 36929, a Psalter in Latin of St. Jerome's Gallican version is the subject of this study, *Secrets of Cistercian Music in Ireland 1142 - 1541 Cistercian Abbey Churches, where the very stones sing the psalms Ireland.* I obtained a copy of it from the British Library and noted mention of men like Jerome, St. Augustine, Bernard, Alcuin, Cassiodorus along with a folio of music, written by Cormac. Unfortunately out of thirty three Cistercian abbeys in Medieval Ireland, we do not know to which it belonged.

In my book "The Impact of the Cistercians on the Landscape of Ireland" I have researched the work of Cistercian monks in agriculture, sheep and cattle rearing, cultivation of crops, land reclamation, the establishment and management of 138 granges, their buildings, exports, imports, their guest houses, fish traps, quarries, hydrology schemes, over a period of circa four hundred years. This is my first time to research 'what went on in the abbey church'. In total, four hours each day, seven days a week, three hundred and sixty five days per year, choir monks proceeded to the abbey church to sing the Divine Office. This was something I wanted to investigate and soon realised that the Cistercian contribution to the field of music was, to say the least, enormous and indeed comparable to their impact on the landscape. They were the foremost men of their time in the field of music.

St. Benedict said Listen my son *Ecoutez mon fil* in the Holy Rule, but Bernard (St.) says in the Song of Songs *Solus qui canta audit*, 'only he who sings hears'. An awareness of music and sound is found in the title of the Cistercian Abbey of Middleton, County Cork, *Chorus Sancti Benedicti* which in the Irish language was Mainistir Na Corann, 'the monastery of the weir' – in which they compared their singing to the music of the water as it passed over the fishing weir, and indeed Kyrie Eleison, the Kyrie of the Mass (i.e. lamb of God) in County Kerry. The bell ringer, who summoned the brethren to the Divine Office and the pealing of the Angelus bell, perhaps inspired by the Latin Cross with three treble strokes and then nine strokes at dawn, midday and at the end of the day after Compline, as well as the funeral bell, all had and still have meaning.

The *Salve Regina* is said to have been composed by St. Bernard, universally recognised and claimed as their great musical possession, held from the Middle Ages and the key signature today of men whose hearts and souls meditate and contemplate the Omnipotent God, *Contemplado Dei*.

Illustration 1
Letter 'A' from the bible commissioned by St. Stephen Harding

Dijon, Bibliotheque municipale.

Chapter 2 | The Cistercian Order and St. Bernard

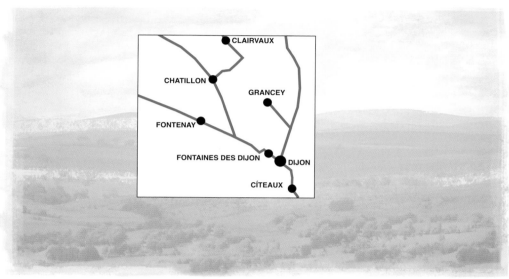

Map 1
Citeaux – routes via Dijon to Citeaux

St. Bernard was born in 1090, at the Chateau of Fontaines. His mother was Aleth of Monthoud and his father, a knight called Bernard Tescalin. Both parents were landowners in the area of Burgundy.[1] He had one sister called Humbeline, and five brothers, Guy, Gerard, Andrew, Bartholomew and Nivard. It is claimed that his mother, a very pious women, taught him to read, and used the psalter as a text. This would remind us of a similar custom in Ireland, as early as the seventh century, Irish children were also taught to read using the psalter as a text on parchment, about seven centuries at least before the invention of the printing press. When it came to his formal education, the family moved from their home, the Chateau of Fontaines, to Chatillon, so that Bernard could attend a school run by the secular canons of St. Vorles [map 1].

It is said that he was very interested in the Bible, in St. Augustine, Bishop of Hippo (396-430) and Boethius [ca.480-524/26], and that he had a great ability for finding the meaning of symbols.

He left school at sixteen and went back to his former home, the Chateau of Fontaines but was very upset when on the following September 1, his mother died. She was a devout woman and was buried in the crypt of the Abbey of St. Bénigne.

Bernard had then to decide on a career. He had two options, either to become a knight like his father, and serve the Duke of Burgundy, or become a priest and for the latter choice, he would have had to go to study in Germany. This was during a period (the eleventh century) when Pope Gregory VII was trying to make the clergy less dependent on secular rulers but the knightly class predominated whilst monastic life was centred on the great Benedictine Abbey of Cluny.

Bernard's father told him that his brothers had gone to support the Duke of Burgundy at the siege of Grancey and they wanted him to meet them near Dijon. This he decided to do. However on the way, he went into a church to pray for direction and decided that he would like to follow a religious life rather than to become a knight. He told this to his uncle Gaudry and thereafter, went to visit Stephen Harding, abbot of a small Cistercian community which had broken from the Benedictine Abbey of Cluny to follow more faithfully the Rule of St. Benedict.

Bernard would have become aware of the great difficulties faced by Stephen Harding and his monks, when they left the Abbey of Molesme. They had been led by a monk called Robert, who followed correct practice by asking Hugh, Archbishop of Lyons who was also the Apostolic Legate of France to obtain from him the necessary approval of ecclesiastical authority. This he received and accompanied by Alberic (the prior) John, Stephen, Laetald and Peter moved out.

There was terrible reaction to this in the Abbey of Molesme, with open violence, particularly against the prior Alberic who as Stephen Harding (St.), an eyewitness, said "suffered much ill treatment, was buffeted and finally imprisoned". Then this group was joined by another fourteen, who were also interested in reform and together they moved southwards to a solitude of Citeaux given to them by Raynald, Viscount of Beaune in the Diocese of Chalons-sur Saone (present day Diocese of Dijon). The Lord of the district was Odo, Duke of Burgundy, and he gave them all that was needed for the erection of the "new monastery" and this began on March 25, 1098, the Feast of St. Benedict.[2]

The Benedictine monks at Molesme were not pleased and in April 1099 sent a delegation to Pope Urban II to order them to return.[3] It so happened that the Pope was presiding at a Council of bishops and abbots and after discussion, he decided to agree to their request and he followed this with a letter to his legate Archbishop Hugh. The latter decided to hold a meeting of local bishops and monks to discuss the matter and it was decided that Robert should go back to the abbey of Molesme and this he did.

After he left, Father Alberic, the prior, was elected Abbot, thereby becoming the second Abbot of Citeaux.[4] He was very prudent, and sent two monks, John and Ilbodus to the new pope, Paschal II to ask for the protection of the Holy See, for the "New Monastery" and this was granted on April 18, 1100 AD. Nine years later, 26 January 1109, Alberic died and his place was taken by Stephen Harding, an Englishman.[5] This was the monk from whom Bernard sought guidance about his vocation. He was born in Dorsetshire, attended the school of the nearby Benedictine priory of Shelbourne, then after the Normans conquered England in 1066, he left to continue his studies in Scotland, or Ireland, where the Benedictines had gone to avoid the war. After that he went for further study in Paris and there he met an Englishman called Peter and when their course was finished they went on a pilgrimage to Rome. On the way they visited the Benedictine Abbey of Molesme, which he later entered, and after a certain time, he became sub prior but as previously mentioned, was one of the twenty-one monks who left.

Bernard (St.) must have been impressed with the Cistercian way of life and decided to enter Citeaux. He was now twenty-two years of age and thirty of his companions made the same decision and also entered. The names of ten of these men are known, Guido, Gerard, Andrew, Bartholomew, Nivard, his mother's two brothers,

Gaudry of Touillon and Mile of Monbard, two cousins, Geoffrey de la Roche and Robert and his three friends, Hugh of Vitry (called Macow), Geoffrey of Ainay and Artaud.

Citeaux was not too far from Bernard's home, the Castle of Fontaines (Chateau of Fontaines) and the entrance of so many local men to Citeaux encouraged many others to enter, with the result that Abbot Stephen had to make new foundations, the first of which was La Ferte, consecrated May 18, 1113, Pontigny in 1114 and in 1115, Bernard was put in charge of a community which included his five brothers, his uncles, his cousins Geoffrey and Robert and five others. This abbey was sited in a deep valley of the River Aube and on its left bank. It was known as the Vallee d'Absinthe – 'Valley of Wormwood' or 'Bitterness', but was changed to 'Clara Vallis', 'Clairvaux' and in the same year another abbey, Morimond, the fourth daughter of Citeaux was founded by Arnold, brother of Archbishop Frederick of Cologne.

Abbot Stephen Harding of Citeaux had great legislative ability and in 1116, he called the four superiors of these abbeys together and a draft document which he had prepared for the future governance of Cistercian monasteries was discussed. Bernard was not at that meeting, he was too ill to attend. Two years later, another meeting was held and the document was again reviewed and this time unanimously accepted. This was the document known as the Charter of Charity.[6] Each abbey was recognised as independent and self governing, presided over by an abbot who was irremovable by higher authority. However, there were two other considerations, namely the holding of General Chapters and regular visitations. The father of a daughter house was required (and is) to visit each monastery every year to examine the administration, the discipline, correct abuses if any, and each monk had to be interviewed on the same occasion, to ascertain if he had any problems or concerns about life in the abbey. The second regulation was that the abbots of the Order were to assemble annually at Citeaux in General Chapter to discuss any matter concerning the Order and it was invested with supreme legislative and executive powers. No monastery was exempt from these rules, not even Abbot Stephen's own monastery of Citeaux. The four abbots of La Ferte, Pontigny, Clairvaux and Morimond were required to visit it in person, unless prevented by sickness.

In 1119 after Pope Callixtus II was elected, he convoked a council at Rheims, then he visited the town of Saulier which is located between Citeaux and La Ferte. Abbot Stephen had drawn up a document which gives an account of the early developments of Citeaux; the Exordium Parvum,[7] and he decided to give it to the Pope. He was received by the latter and on December 23, 1119 and on that occasion, he asked that the Charter of Charity should be sanctioned. Approval was given and the canonical existence of the Order was established.

During Abbot Stephen Harding's administration, the compilation of the *Liber Usuum* was undertaken (between 1120 and 1125). The Rule of St. Benedict gives exact prescription concerning the Divine Office, the Opus Dei and the daily routine of the life in the monastery. This was also regulated and is now found in the "Book of Customs"[8] [the Consuetudines], the aim of which is to preserve uniformity. Special attention was laid on the perfect execution of the Divine Office, by the Charter of Charity which decreed that "all our monasteries have the same books for the Office". The books of the Order at that time were *Regula St. Benedicti, Liber Usuum, [Consuetudines], Psalterium, Hymnarium Collectaneum, Lectionarium,*

Antiphonarium and Gradule. Each mother house had to furnish its daughter houses with the necessary transcripts and no colony could be sent out to found a new abbey without a complete set of them.

This is important to note, as the first French monks who came to Ireland (see Ch. 3) would have brought these with them from France and from them transcriptions[9] for use in the abbeys for growing communities were made.

Stephen Harding also wanted to provide a Bible for each of his monasteries, and obtained copies from several monasteries, hoping to find a satisfactory text. However there were so many variants, he produced a new revised edition. He obtained help from some learned rabbis in the Troyes area and succeeded in re-establishing the Latin text of the Old Testament books in close conformity with the Hebrew and Chaldean texts. This is the Great Bible of Citeaux which is kept in the Municipal Library of Dijon. At the end of it, there is a note, which reads: "In the year 1109 of the Incarnation of our Lord, this Book was completed while Stephen, second Abbot of the Monastery of Citeaux was ruling". There is also a concluding note requesting "that those reading it, should not make any corrections into the text, nor to erase any of those that have been entered". Then he cautions against the careless handling of a work that has required so much painstaking labour.[10]

In 1133, after being abbot for twenty five years, Stephen at the General Chapter, resigned, and his place was taken by Guido, a monk of Bernard's monastery of Clairvaux. When Stephen died in 1133, there were seventy abbeys, twenty years later when Bernard died, there were 343 abbeys, sixty five of which had been founded from Bernard's monastery of Clairvaux.

In 1133 Bernard became the chief propagator of the Cistercian Order and it will be shown in Chapter 3 that it was he who advised his close friend Malachy, Archbishop of Armagh, to introduce the Order to Ireland with the founding of Mellifont Abbey in 1142.

Illustration 1a contd. ms13f. 150v (Colophon de la Bible). "that those reading it should not make any corrections into the text nor to erase any of those that have been entered"

Dijon, Bibliotheque municipale.

Chapter 3 | Clairvaux founds Irish houses, French monks arrive in Ireland

> *"For although they did not come from our house in particular, still coming from a daughter house of ours"*
>
> **Letter 545 Codex 291, Vienna**

In 1139 Malachy went to Rome to ask for the pallia for the archbishops of Armagh and Cashel. With him were some companions. The journey to Rome was difficult. Leaving from Bangor (County Down) they crossed the Irish Sea, to England, then over to France and southwards through that country to Rome. It has been estimated that such a journey took nine months. On their way they stayed at St. Bernard's monastery, Clairvaux. Whilst there, Malachy was so taken with the life lived by the monks, he wanted to become a Cistercian himself. However he and his party continued their journey to meet Pope Innocent II in Rome. Malachy asked the Pope if he might resign his position as bishop in Ireland to become a Cistercian monk, but the Pope refused. Instead he made him Papal Legate to Ireland. Regarding the pallia, the Pope told Malachy to go back to Ireland and call a meeting of churchmen, to make arrangements to have Ireland divided into four archbishoprics rather than two.

On his return journey to Ireland, Malachy again stayed with Bernard at Clairvaux and discussed his visit to the Pope with him. The latter then advised Malachy to bring the Cistercian Order to Ireland saying:

> *Go and with the wisdom given onto you*
> *Prepare a site similar to what you have seen*
> *Far removed from the turmoil of the world.*

Malachy accepted the suggestion and left four of his companions with St. Bernard to be trained as monks.

On his return to Ireland, Malachy approached his friend Donnchad O'Cearbhail for a land grant. Malachy negotiated with him and moved the boundary line of the Armagh Diocese from Slieve Breagh (which was a mountain ridge which ran from Clogher Head to Drogheda) to the mid-water of the River Boyne. This made the southern boundary of the Diocese of Armagh co-terminous with the kingdom of Airghialla. In this newly acquired territory, O'Cearbhail gave the land grant for Mellifont Abbey [see map 2]. In due course St. Bernard sent a monk named Robert from his own Abbey of Clairvaux to take charge of building the new abbey.

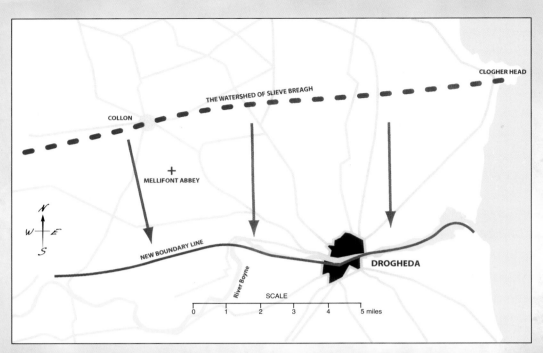

Map 2 *Diocesan Boundary Change made by St. Malachy for Mellifont Abbey, County Louth*

The question as to where the monks lived whilst the abbey was being built has never been raised nor debated. However, Monasterboice, one mile from the Mellifont site (as the crow flies) had been vacant from 1122 and perhaps with some temporary wooden buildings may have been used. It was part of Mellifont's possessions, and on the foundation land grant given by O'Cearbhail [see map 3].

Map 3
*The Charter
Lands of
Mellifont Abbey
in County Louth*

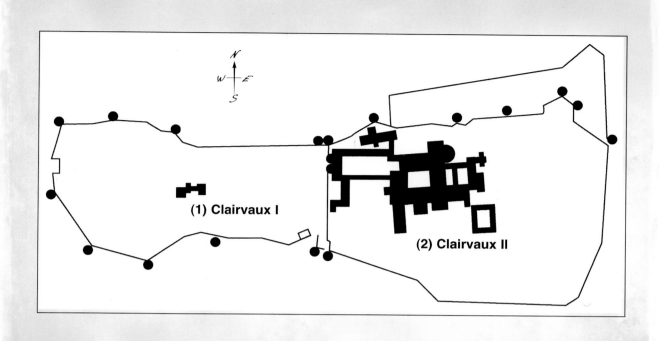

Map 4
Site of St. Bernard's Monastery from Clairvaux I to Clairvaux II.
*The first work undertaken by the Cistercians when building a monastery
was to excavate the site and lay the water systems*

The site at Mellifont *far from the haunts of man*, was very restricted, it was in a cul-de-sac on the River Mattock, a meandering stream of low density, tributary to the River Boyne [see photo]. However the French architect monk from Clairvaux would have had knowledge of site problems, as the monastery of Clairvaux had experienced difficulties and had to move from their first choice site eastwards, thereby establishing Clairvaux II [see map 4].

It was decided to build Mellifont Abbey on the left bank of the Mattock River, but the standard plan brought from Clairvaux was more suitable for a right bank site. Subsequently, twenty-five of the thirty-three Cistercian abbeys were sited on the right banks of rivers, whether on a first[11] or second order stream.[12] The tendency to choose the right bank may have had its origin in early monastic sites in Egypt. It is known that in AD 285 Anthony, the father of monasticism, crossed the River Nile and walked to a place called Pispir on the right bank [see map 5] where he established a hermitage. Three hundred miles south of Pispir and five hundred miles south of the Nitran desert Pachomius decided to build a cell for himself in a deserted village called Tabennisi on the east bank of the Nile. When that became too congested he built another monastery at Pebook three or four miles to the north and likewise on the right bank of the Nile [see map 5].

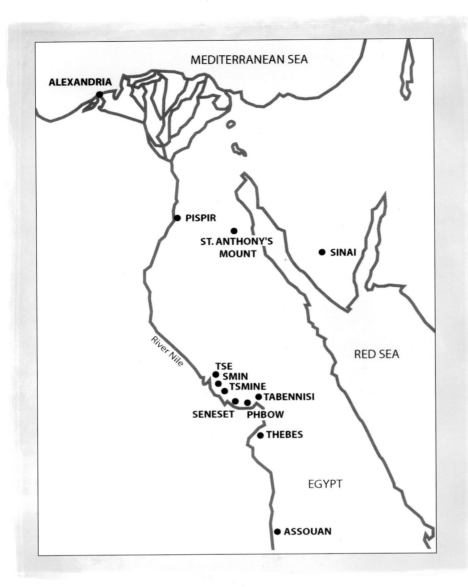

MEDITERRANEAN SEA

ALEXANDRIA

PISPIR

ST. ANTHONY'S
MOUNT

SINAI

River Nile

RED SEA

TSE
SMIN
TSMINE
TABENNISI
SENESET   PHBOW

THEBES

EGYPT

ASSOUAN

Map 5
EGYPT 'The Right Bank'
*Monastic sites on the Right
Bank of the River Nile
(In passing it is worth noting
that Nunneries were sited on
the left bank).*

Cistercian abbeys needed water for domestic purposes and for water power. The most desirable water power situation was one where a tributary stream with a relatively steep gradient joined a main stream, from which an artificial watercourse could be engineered, passing first of all along the southern side of the cloistral complex and if possible from west to east so as to pass the refectory and kitchen before reaching the rere dorter at the end of the monk's house. This was not possible at the site for Mellifont Abbey, since the Mattock follows a meandering course [see map 3 and photo 6].

G Carville

G Carville

Photo 1 & 2
A close-up photo of a conduit. It is claimed that Mellifont Abbey made bricks as well as tiles

10

The right bank of the River Mattock is steep, with an overburden of fifty feet (approx.) of boulder clay. Furthermore it is in County Meath whilst the left bank is in County Louth. The left bank had an outcrop of Silurian grits (sandstones) and slates. This had to be excavated to a depth of approximately twenty feet. There is a slope extending for thirty-four and a half feet from the west end of the church towards the east of considerable depth and a crypt of twelve feet (approx.) had to be built under the west end of the church. During periods of very heavy rainfall, the Mattock has flooded the land on the left bank, including the crypt. Mellifont Abbey occupies a quarry site; there are surface rock exposures visible in the former day stairs area, and in the kitchen area [see photo 4].

G Carville

Photo 3
The Lavabo Mellifont Abbey, a two storey building with windows in the upper floor

Photo 4
Rock outcrops which show the challenge that the builders of Mellifont Abbey had to overcome to excavate this site. These were below floor level outcrops and were not cut away. Notice the replacement wall to give a square-ended church

G Carville

This type of rock, Silurian grits and sandstone, has a low permeability, it does not allow large quantities of water to move through it and wells are usually low yielding and is classified as a poor aquifer. The Cistercian architect/engineers always cut the necessary watercourses before any building was undertaken. Here the nature of the bedrock does not allow water to move through it readily, with the result that seeps, rises and small springs are common, particularly at changes in slope. On the hillside overlooking the eastern range of buildings, watercourses devised by the early builders can be seen in the form of shore drains and there is a 'moat-like structure/reservoir' whereby streams and springs were intercepted and engineered to flow into this 'reservoir' and thereafter via a conduit into the kitchen of the abbey. Another led to the Lavabo, after all 'cleanliness was inherent in Cistercian aesthetics'. The Lavabo would have had in the middle a circular basin from which water never ceased to flow [see photo 3].[13]

The perfect monastery was evolved in Clairvaux and rapidly became the norm. Abbots of other foreign monasteries came to send their architects to Clairvaux to take the precise measurements of their paradigm. Aubert says that Abbot Wigbold from the Dutch monastery of Aduard sent a lay brother to Burgundy for this purpose in 1224. This lay brother did such a perfect job of building the monastery and its church that he was accorded the rare honour of a burial place before the High Altar.[14]

During the building of Mellifont Abbey, the French architect/engineer monk Robert went back to his own monastery of Clairvaux. Perhaps he returned to study some aspect of its buildings but unfortunately this has led to conjecture that there was a clash of French/Irish temperament or that something went wrong relating to the work in progress that made him return. No doubt St. Bernard discussed the problems with him when he arrived at Clairvaux but there does not seem to have been acrimony, because when St. Bernard asked him to come back to Ireland to continue the work, he acceded to Bernard's request *like an obedient son.*

Robert must have been concerned about the limits of the site; there was no available passage or lane to the exterior of the east range. The presence of a high-rise bank, which would have required further rock cutting, was a physical obstacle to providing one [see photo 6].

As the buildings rose, Malachy was anxious to have the postulants whom he had left with Bernard for training as Cistercian monks sent back to Mellifont Abbey. However the latter told Malachy in a letter that he should wait:

> *Quod autem voluistis duos de fratribus mitte vobis ad praevidendum*
> *locum, communicato cum fratribus consilo, dignam duximus non eos*
> *separandos ab invicem, Donec plenius in eis Formetur Christas donec*
> *ad integrum doceantur procliari proelia Domini ...*[15]

This letter was written c.1137, so this period of three years was insufficient for their formation. Eventually in 1142, four postulants after approximately five years of training arrived in Mellifont. One was called Christian and he was from a district called Conor hence Christian O Connairche, but he was sent back again to make *further observances.* In due course he did return to Mellifont Abbey, as Abbot.

River Mattock

Photo 6
*The Mattock River is of low density but the Cistercians obtained the water for domestic purposes from a
moat / reservoir which they constructed on the raised ground behind the abbey.*

The foundation of Mellifont Abbey was very successful and before Malachy's death in 1148, five daughter houses were founded, Bective 1147, Inishlounaght 1147, Boyle 1148, Monasternenagh 1148, Baltinglass 1148, but how was this possible? Regarding personnel twelve monks and an abbot were needed for each foundation, therefore sixty-five were required along with a similar number of lay brothers. This remained a puzzle for me until I read of two recently discovered letters of Bernard by a Dutch Dominican scholar Rev. G.G. Meerseman OP in Codex 291 of the Black Friars at Vienna.[16] Now follows a print of one of those letters,[17] Letter DXLV – Letter 545 from St. Bernard to St. Malachy, followed by one in which the Latin text is established and that in turn by an English language translation of the same.

EPISTOLA DXLV
Epistola confraternitatis ad Malachiam legatum Hiberniae

Illustration 2
Text in Medieval Latin - Letter 545 and Letter 546

Magno sacerdoti et summo amico suo Malachiae, Apostolicae Sedis legato, frater Bernardus, Claraevallis vocatus abbas : salutem et orationem.

Licet longe sitis a nobis, non tamen ab animo nostro longe estis, quia locorum vel temporum incommoda sanctus amor ignorat. Vasto siquidem mari distinguimur, sed coniungimur caritate. Caritas enim in sacrario dilectionis amplectitur, quam nec Oceanus, nec aquae multae poterunt extinguere, nec illam flumina obruere. In hac ergo semper vobiscum sum, per hanc vos semper mecum estis. Quomodo enim non diligerem in Christo Domino eum cui scientia ad doctrinam, vita ad conscientiam, mores ad exemplum plenissime, ut audivimus, suffragantur? Super omnia autem coniunxit me vobis filiorum et tratrum nostrorum, qui nuper ad partes illas perrexerunt, benigna susceptio, quos fovetis, quos diligitis, quos efficaciter iuvatis. Licet enim de domo nostra specialiter non exstiterint, tamen de filia domus nostrae non minus dilecti, quia omnes, et longe et prope, unum sumus in Christo, et hos et illos, qui de latere nostro ad vos venerint, vestrae paternitati specialius commendamus, supplicantes ut, quod bene coepistis, melius consummetis in Domino. Et ut hoc libentius faciatis, participem vos facimus omnium bonorum quae fiunt et fient in ordine nostro usque in sempiternum.

TRANSLATION OF LETTER 545
Letter of brotherhood to Malachy Legate of Ireland

To the great priest and most special friend Malachy, legate of the Apostolic See, brother Bernard, styled Abbot of Clairvaux : health and prayer.

    Although you are far from us, nevertheless you are not far from our mind, because holy love ignores obstacles of places or times. Indeed we are separated by a vast sea, but we are united by charity. For charity embraces in the holy place of love (charity) which neither the Ocean nor many waters could quench, nor rivers overwhelm. In this (charity) therefore I am always with you, through this you are always with me. For how would I not love in Christ the Lord, him in whom knowledge most fully avails for doctrine, life for conscientiousness, moral life for (good) example as we have heard. *Above all however your kindly welcome of our sons and brothers who lately went to those parts unites me to you. You cherish them, you love them, you help them effectively. For although they did not come from our house in particular, still coming from a daughter house of our house they are not less beloved (by us), because we all, far and near, are one in Christ and we more especially commend to your paternity (fatherly care) both these*[18] *and those*[19] *who came to you from our side, beseeching (you) that what you have begun well you may better bring to completion in the Lord.* And that you may do this more willingly we make you sharers in all the good which is done and will be done in our Order forever.

EPISTOLA DXLVI
Epistola Confraternitatis ad Dyernetium Hiberniae regem.

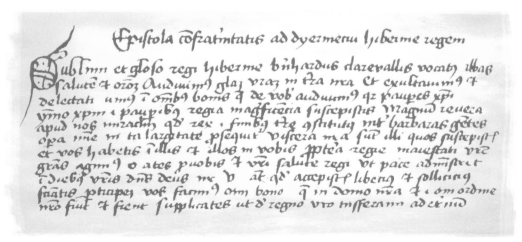

Audivimus gloriam vestram in terra nostra, et exsultavimus, quia pauperes Christi, immo Christum in pauperibus regia magnificentia suscepistis. Magnum revera apud nos miraculum, quod rex in finibus terrae constitutus inter barbaras gentes opera

misericordiae multa largitate prosequitur. Viscera nostra sunt illi quos suscepistis, et nos habetis in illis et illos in nobis. Propterea regiae maiestati vestrae gratias agimus, orantespro vobis et pro vestri salute regni, ut pacem administret in diebus vestris Dominus Deus noster. Ut autem quod coepistis, libentius et sollicitius finiatis, participem vos facimus omnium bonorum quae in domo nostra et in omni ordine nostro fiunt et fient, supplicantes ut de regno terreno transferamini ad aeternum.

Our very intimate selves are those whom you have received, and you have us in them and them in us.

Letter of brotherhood to Dermot King of Ireland
[Dermot II, King of Ireland, who in the year 1148 gave land to the monks of the Abbey of Mellifont to found there, the monastery of Vallis Salutis]

To the sublime and glorious King of Ireland, Bernard, styled Abbot of Clairvaux: health and prayer.

We have heard (of) your glory in our land, and we have rejoiced because with kingly magnificence you have received the poor of Christ – even more: Christ in the poor. Truly (it is) a great miracle among us that a king *set among barbarous nations* in the ends of the earth follows up works of mercy with much generosity. Our very intimate selves *are those whom you have received*, and you have us in them and them in us. Wherefore we give thanks to your royal majesty, praying for you and for the safety of your kingdom that the Lord our God will bestow peace in your days. Now that what you have begun you may more willingly and carefully bring to its completion, we make you partaker of all the good which is done and will be done in our house and in our whole Order, beseeching that from an earthly kingdom you may be raised to the Eternal.

[Recueil II 316, N10; Jan 114-115 ("Jan": L. Janauschek, *Originum Cisterciensium* 1, Vienna, 1877); G. Carville, "The Cistercian Settlement of Ireland (1142-1541)" in *Studia Monastica*, p.31.]

This is a very important letter, as it states that French monks *from a daughter house came to Ireland* and helped in setting up Mellifont Abbey's five foundations, and would have required at least sixty-five monks. St. Bernard also thanks Malachy for his *kindness and hospitality and for the efficient arrangements he made for them.* One can also say that when the French monk Robert returned to Clairvaux during the building of Mellifont Abbey, he must have given a favourable opinion of those Irish with whom he had become acquainted otherwise it is unlikely that an influx of monks *from Clairvaux's daughter house* would have come to Ireland, either to Mellifont or to

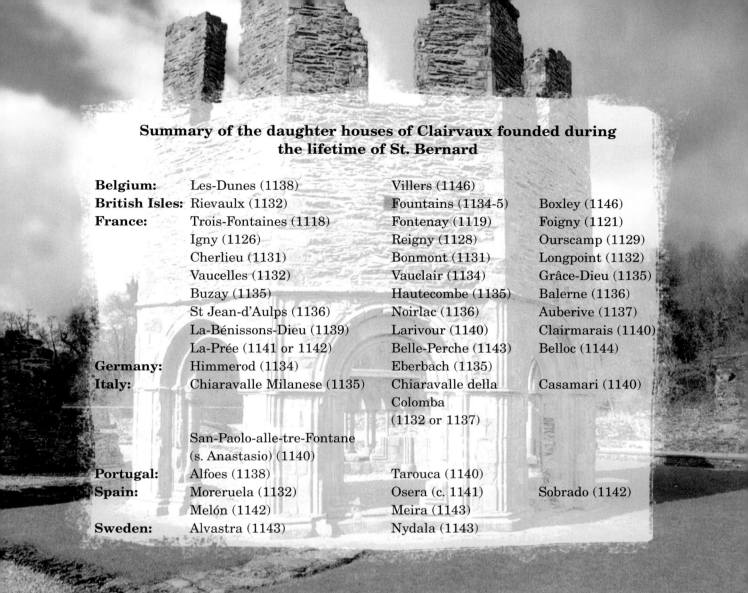

Summary of the daughter houses of Clairvaux founded during the lifetime of St. Bernard

Belgium:	Les-Dunes (1138)	Villers (1146)	
British Isles:	Rievaulx (1132)	Fountains (1134-5)	Boxley (1146)
France:	Trois-Fontaines (1118)	Fontenay (1119)	Foigny (1121)
	Igny (1126)	Reigny (1128)	Ourscamp (1129)
	Cherlieu (1131)	Bonmont (1131)	Longpoint (1132)
	Vaucelles (1132)	Vauclair (1134)	Grâce-Dieu (1135)
	Buzay (1135)	Hautecombe (1135)	Balerne (1136)
	St Jean-d'Aulps (1136)	Noirlac (1136)	Auberive (1137)
	La-Bénissons-Dieu (1139)	Larivour (1140)	Clairmarais (1140)
	La-Prée (1141 or 1142)	Belle-Perche (1143)	Belloc (1144)
Germany:	Himmerod (1134)	Eberbach (1135)	
Italy:	Chiaravalle Milanese (1135)	Chiaravalle della Colomba (1132 or 1137)	Casamari (1140)
	San-Paolo-alle-tre-Fontane (s. Anastasio) (1140)		
Portugal:	Alfoes (1138)	Tarouca (1140)	
Spain:	Moreruela (1132)	Osera (c. 1141)	Sobrado (1142)
	Melón (1142)	Meira (1143)	
Sweden:	Alvastra (1143)	Nydala (1143)	

any of her daughter houses. The coming of these monks enabled the expansion of Mellifont's new foundations. Bernard also mentions *the departure of monks for those places* (regions), in other words the French monks were not confined to only one of Mellifont's daughter houses.

Related to the arrival of these monks, the question arises as to which of Bernard's daughter houses did they come? How many daughter houses had Clairvaux before this letter was written to Malachy c.1147. In France, there were twenty-four, two in Germany, four in Italy, two in Portugal, six in Spain, two in Sweden but it is probable that they came from one of the French abbeys.[20]

In 1147 Malachy called a Council meeting of Irish clergy at Inis Padraig, near Dublin, to discuss the setting up of four archbishoprics in Ireland. A decision was taken that Malachy should go to Rome to Pope Eugenius for the palluim for each archbishop and he went. He was now fifty-four years old, again he called with Bernard at Clairvaux but fell ill and died 1st November 1148.

Bernard wrote an account of the *Life of St. Malachy* and a cult developed, both in France and Ireland. In 1708 an English Benedictine monk Milley drew the following plan of "The Grange of Outre-Aube with the gate towards the forest, and

Saint Malachie fountain; the Rue de La Fontaine-Saint Malachie which flows into the Aube, 220 yards further on, the grange with five aisles and grange of seven aisles, the house of the grange master and the lay brothers, the agricultural buildings, the gate house and guest house and enclosing wall"[21]

The Grange of Outre-Aube

A. Gate towards the forest and Saint-Malachie fountain.

B. Rue de la Fontaine Saint-Malachie.

C. Grange with five aisles (burned down in 1986), and the Grange of seven aisles visible on the aerial photograph taken by raking light.

D. The house of the Grange-master and the lay brothers, still standing, but altered.

E. Agricultural buildings, one still standing but altered.

F. Gate-house and guest-house, existing but altered.

G. Enclosing wall.

From Dom Millery (1708) and Viollet-le-Duc

From the map drawn by J R Leroux L'Abbey de Clairvaux La Vie en Champafne 1986

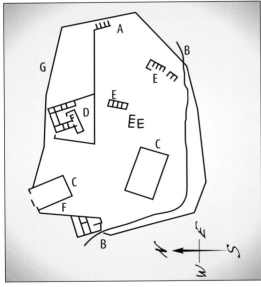

Map 6
The Grange of Outre-Aube

B Quinn

Photo 7 - On the Grange of Outre-Aube, Clairvaux, France

This grange was eight miles from the Abbey of Clairvaux and is where Malachy and his companions left the main route on their way to Rome[22] to rest. For architect Robert and the monks from the daughter house of Clairvaux the remains of Mellifont, Baltinglass, Bective, Inishlounaght, Monasternenagh and Boyle on the landscape of Ireland are indelibly stamped with the undeniable truth of their presence, as is the grange of Malachy, Bar-sur-Aube on the landscape of France.

This same plan or layout was used in 742 Cistercian Abbeys in Medieval Europe.

Duchas

Photo 8 - Holy Cross Abbey. A house full of books, music, light and psalms.

St. Bernard was greatly influenced in his theological formation by St. Augustine. Wilmart, writing about the wide distribution of his works in the Middle Ages, noted that in the library at Troyes (MS32) there is the remains of the twelfth century catalogue of the library of Clairvaux. It contained the first part of the *Retractions De trinitate De Musica De Verá religione* along with works by Boethius (including the commentary by William of Conches), Johannes Scotus Erigena, Hugh of St. Victor and Alani Cisterciensis. Dom Wilmart points out that this refutes the legend of the paucity of books in Cistercian libraries. The collection at Clairvaux was undoubtedly created by St. Bernard himself.

La bibliotheque de Clairvaux

telle que nous la voyons au term du XIIe siecle, ne peut qu'etre la creation du premier abbé de Clairvaux il a dû lui-meme fixer le programme selon lequel elle s'est peu a peu organisée et achévee

Wilmart, L'Ancienne Bibliotheque de Clairvaux.[23]

In his Treatise, Augustine "meditates on the mystery of redemption, by which the death of Christ atoned for man's twofold death of body and through sin of soul". As Augustine ponders this congruence, this correspondence, this consonance of one and two, musical experience takes hold of his imagination and suddenly he realises that harmony is the proper term for Christ's work of reconciliation. This is not the place, Augustine exclaims, to demonstrate the value of the octave that seems so deeply implanted in our nature by whom, if not by Him who created us? that even the musically and mathematically uneducated, respond to it. Augustine feels that the consonance of the octave, the musical expression of the ratio 1:2 conveys even to human ears the meaning of the mystery of redemption.[24]

In the second book of his treatise, On Order, Augustine describes how reason in her quest for the blissful contemplation of things divine turns to music and from music to what lies between the range of vision beholding earth and heaven, she realises that only beauty can ever satisfy her, in beauty *figures*, in figures *proportion* and in proportion *number*. Augustine was nearly as sensitive to architecture as he was to music. For him music and architecture are sisters, since both are children of number, they have equal dignity in as much as architecture mirrors eternal harmony, music echoes it.[25]

Boethius further elaborated Augustinian aesthetics, he confined the entire creative process from the first design to the completed composition, within the rigid limits not only of metaphysical doctrine but of certain mathematical laws. Boethius refers to a cube, since the number of its surfaces, angles and edges 6:8:12 contain the ratios of octave, fifth and fourth.[26]

The arithmetic formula; between 6 and 12 is 3, the arithmetic mean is 9 (6 + 3) and (12 − 3) 9.
The harmonic mean 6, 8, 12: 8 - 6 = 2, 12 - 8 = 4, 6 ÷ 2 = 3, 12 ÷ 4 = 3.
The AM (3) equals the HM (3).
6:8:12, 6:8 i.e. 3:4 the perfect 4th, 8:12 i.e. 2:3 the perfect 5th, 6:12 i.e. 1:2 the octave.

In the following passage, Boethius tells how Pythagoras discovered the Ratios of the Consonances:

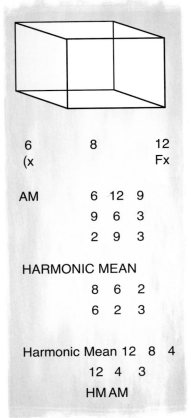

Boethius: The Cube – six surfaces, eight angles, twelve edges. This shows visible and audible harmonies.

"For some time Pythagoras was seeking a way to acquire, through reason, full and accurate knowledge of the criteria for consonances. In the meantime by a kind of divine will, while passing the workshop of blacksmiths, he overheard

the beating of hammers somehow emit a single consonance from differing sounds. Thus in the presence of what he had long sought, he approached the activity spellbound. Reflecting for a time he decided that the strength of the men hammering caused the diversity of sounds and in order to prove this more clearly, he commanded them to exchange hammers among themselves. But the property of sounds did not rest in the muscles of the men; rather it followed the exchanged hammers. When he observed this, he examined the weight of the hammers. There happened to be five hammers and those that sounded together the consonance of the octave were found to be double in weight. Pythagoras determined further that the one which weighed twice the second was in the ratio 4:3 with another with which it sounded a diatessaron (fourth). Then he found that the same double of the second formed the ratio 3:2 with still another, and that it joined with it in the consonance of the diapente (fifth)."[27]

Augustine's authority shaped the Middle Ages, "thou hast created all things in measure and number and weight", and the interpretation that Augustine gave this became the keyword of the medieval world view. Number and composition led to the development of medieval music and equally showed this in architecture.

Bernard adopted Augustine's ideas. Perfect proportions determined by rigid geometrical considerations became a technical necessity, as well as an aesthetic ideal, if the building was to be stable as well as beautiful. The Cistercian style of architecture which developed under Bernard is renowned. The extent of his supervision is not known but the monk Archardus, built under his direction, *Archardus ... jubente et millente beato Bernardo ... plurimorum cenenobiorum initiator et extructor*. When the French architect Robert was working on the Mellifont site, Ireland, he was faced with problems, and returned to Bernard in Clairvaux to discuss them.

Villard de Honnecourt was an architect from Picardy, who was trained on site at the Cistercian monastery of Vauclair, a daughter house of Clairvaux. Fortunately his notebook is extant and in it there is a plan for "a Cistercian church of the Order of Citeaux". This does not necessarily mean that he was the originator of this plan, but possessed a standard one, approved for any Cistercian monastic church. "This is a church made up of squares which has to be erected for the Order of Citeaux". Otto von Simpson in his study on the Gothic Cathedral, says that (St.) Bernard contributed to the spiritual foundations of the new style. The true characteristics of Gothic architecture lay in the use of light and the harmony of structural elements based on 'true measure', expressed in geometrical equations which echoed Pythagorean and Neoplatonic mysticism. Any church laid out on that system will have ratios 1:1, 1:2, 3:4 which correspond to St. Augustine's musical harmonics. Augustine's perfect ratio of squares and cubes is a conspicuous feature of its design, each aisle bay is a square in plan and each square is made into a cube in as much as the height of the vault is the same as the width of the aisle.[28]

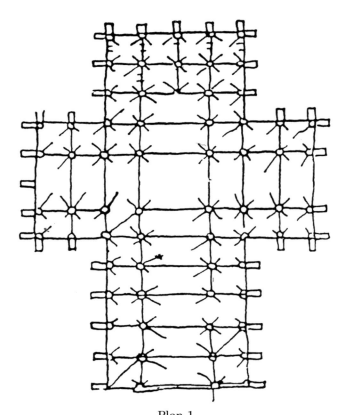

Plan 1
This is a church made up of squares which was to be erected for the order of Citeaux. From the notebook of Villard de Honnecourt.
Francois Bucher - Cistercian architectural purism
(with permission)

The question arises as to what exactly this means, regarding architecture, other than the throw away observation of 'square ended' or 'straight ended' churches. How can these musical consonances be related to architecture? To show this I related these proportions of Villard de Honnecourt's plan for the "church for the Order of Citeaux" to the tonal scale as follows (see diagram) and in this way proved Otto von Simpson's observation and Bernard's desire, based on Augustinian ideas that the ratio of the chords in music would give perfect symmetry and harmony to the Cistercian architectural plan.

Duchas

Photo 9 - *Window, Holy Cross Abbey, Co. Tipperary*

St. Bernard paid great attention to the construction of abbeys and employed the best architects of his day.

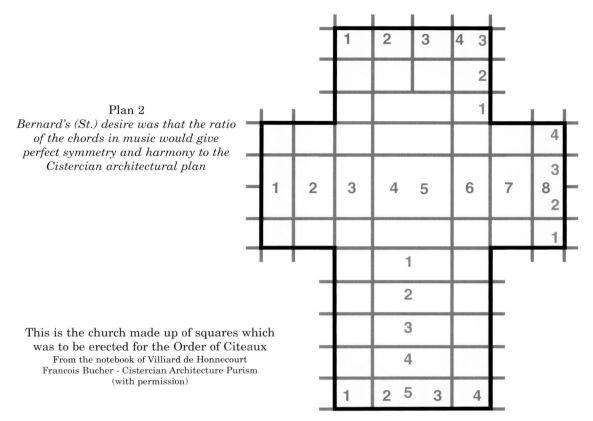

Plan 2
Bernard's (St.) desire was that the ratio of the chords in music would give perfect symmetry and harmony to the Cistercian architectural plan

This is the church made up of squares which was to be erected for the Order of Citeaux
From the notebook of Villiard de Honnecourt
Francois Bucher - Cistercian Architecture Purism
(with permission)

Musical proportions that correspond to the intervals of the perfect consonances

OVERTONES OF C

Perfect 8ve   Perfect 5th   Perfect 4th   3rd

Sturman P. and Catholic encyclodaedia

Length of Church : Length of Transept 8:12	= 2:3 [C-G]	
		= musical 5th perfect 5th
Width of side aisle and nave	1:2	= octave ratio
Length / width of transept 8/4	1:2	= octave ratio
The choir	3:4	= musical fourth perfect 4th
The nave and side aisles as a unit	4:5	= the musical 3rd
The Crossing	1:1	= the unison
		most perfect of consonances

Hahnloser, A. Reinle and Hanno Hahn, were researchers who studied the proportions in some abbey ruins. Regarding the Villard de Honnecourt plan, Hahnloser characterised the idea for that building on measures based on the width of the crossing as an ideal plan (see plan). A. Reinle composed a series of ordnances deriving from the triple ratio of the so called *Golden Rule. They are as follows:

40:	80:	120	breadth of the nave:	breadth of the nave and aisles:	length of the transept
80:	100:	180	breadth of the nave and aisles:	length of the cloister:	length of the nave
120:	180:	300	length of the transept:	length of the nave:	length of the whole church

This table can be read horizontally or vertically. Such proportions not only reveal the will to absolute harmony but also a spiritual approach that sought a religious symbol in every number. Three times three in the above table pointed to the Trinity and the horizontal and vertical the cross appeared to eyes used to the *carmina figurata*, the emblematic verse of the age.[29]

The unit employed in setting out was the pole, literally a pole. There was no national standard of length. The surveyors could not multiply 2 x 2 without the use of a chequer board, for Arabic numerals were three centuries away. It has been said that each master builder cut his own pole and in doing so varied the interpretation of the linear foot.[30] Thus the size of abbey churches could have been fortuitously related to the length of the pole selected by the surveyor, or the surveyor in making his selection of a pole of certain length may have been guided by a maximum size of abbey plan based on the cost of the project. The Roman foot was 29.57 cms, the Carolingian was 33.29 cms, the French Pied Royale was 32.48 cms, the Anglo Saxon 12 inches. The French Pied Royale of 32.48 cms used in Burgundy corresponds to the 12 inch Anglo Saxon foot. A few modern studies have been carried out to ascertain which if any of these measures were used in Ireland. However there are difficulties, the difference between the Carolingian foot and the Pied Royale is slight, only 0.81 cms and furthermore one would presume that such measurements would be taken in the foundation trenches, the place from which the initial layout was made, before the walls were raised, so far excavations in Ireland have not afforded this opportunity. According to Braun it was customary to stop sixteen men as they entered the church and make each place his foot behind that of his neighbour in order to assess the local pole. Nevertheless the fact that the Cistercians demanded strict uniformity in their monasteries and that the layout of the Cistercian monastery was determined by a standard plan to which all houses were supposed to adhere makes it most unlikely that the size of their abbey churches was fortuitously related to the size of the pole adopted by the surveyor.

*Golden section - 'The division of a line so that one segment is to the other as that is to the whole'.

Ideal Cistercian Monastery (as presented by Aubert & Dimier)

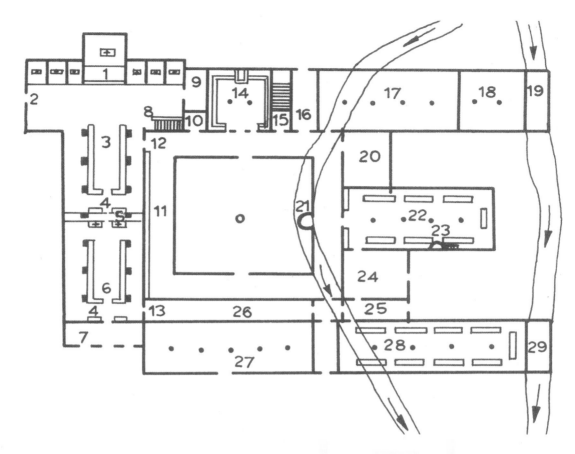

Quod siquis contra statuta capituli ..... edificare presumpserit remota onni dispensatione edificia cadant, expense et opera hereant.

But if anyone shall presume to build in contempt of the statutes of the Chapter, these buildings shall come down without any pardon, and the expense and labour shall be in vain - C31.

Medieval Cistercian monasteries were constructed in the form of a quadrangle around an open space, the Church being on the north side (see plan). Surrounding this central space was the cloister, an arcaded gallery with a lean-to-roof communicating with the different parts of the monastery. The northern walk of the cloister (no.11) which generally extended the length of the nave of the church as far as the south transept was provided with benches for reading and was called the reading cloister. Eastern walk extended southwards from the angle of the nave and the southern transept and parallel to the east range of buildings. Nearest to the church was the sacristy (no.9) then came the library (no.10) the chapter house (no.14) the parlour (no.16) where the monks engaged in necessary conversation with their superior and the Scriptorium or community room (no.17). The monks' dormitory was generally located on the first floor over the whole eastern range and was connected directly with the church via a staircase known as the night stairs since it was used by the monks for the purpose of coming from the dormitory to the church for the night office.

Turning west at the end of the eastern cloister one found oneself in the southern cloister which ran alongside the south range of the monastic buildings. This range contained the calefactory (no. 20) or warming room at the eastern end, the refectory or dining hall of the monks (no. 22) generally known as the Frater, in the center and the kitchen at the western end (no. 24). Opposite the door of the refectory was located the Lavabo (no. 21) which opened out of the cloister. Here was the fountain at which the brethren washed their hands before entering the refectory for meals.

The west range of the monastery extended from the church in the north to the kitchen in the south. This range included the cellar (no.27) and the lay brothers refectory (no. 28) whilst the dorter of the conversi or lay brothers, extended over the whole range (no. 27-28).

The pole was used for setting out the church upon a grid, four poles wide, the main span occupying two of these and the transepts projecting one bay outside the aisle wall, making an overall width of 6 poles. According to Braun, a centre line was marked out (A) [see plan] and the outline of the nave set out two poles length on either side of this (C) giving an overall width of sixty four feet. The outer face of the west wall was then marked out across these two lines (D) and its thickness set out. Nine poles away to the east the length of the nave was marked out (E) and again the thickness of the wall was set out on the farther side of this. The side walls of the nave were then marked out internally within the four pole limit (F). The centre lines of the nave arcade were then set out two poles apart (G) and their width lined up. The nine bays of the nave were set out across these lines.

Plan 4
Design according to Braun

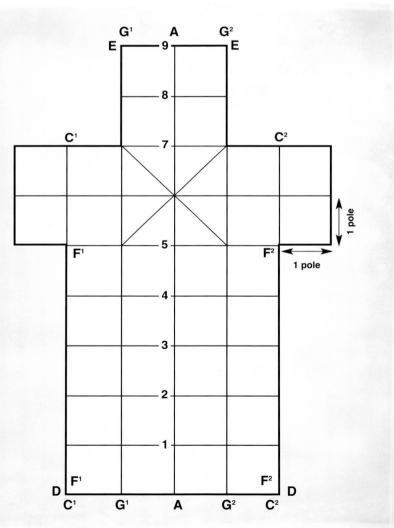

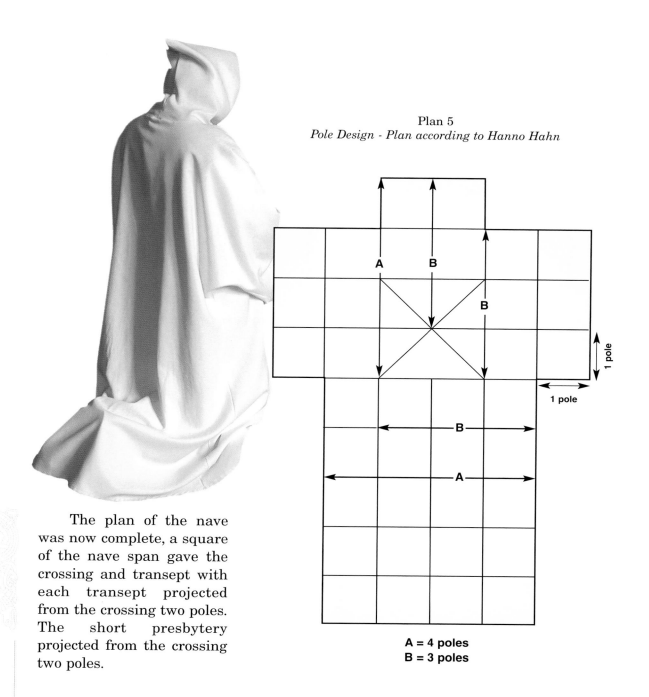

1 pole

1 pole

A = 4 poles
B = 3 poles

The plan of the nave was now complete, a square of the nave span gave the crossing and transept with each transept projected from the crossing two poles. The short presbytery projected from the crossing two poles.

On the other hand, Hanno Hahn who worked on Irish abbey sites has shown that Cistercian churches frequently embody a simple proportional system, involving two related squares. According to Hahn the larger square had a side measure which was determined by the overall width of the transepts and their chapels and it also coincided with the distance from the middle point of the crossing to the east wall of the presbytery, and as the total width of the nave and aisles is 4 poles, hence a ratio of 3:4 (the perfect 4th in musical terms) [see plan]. It would be wrong to impute to medieval building practices our own notions of a highly specialised professionalism. However, knowledge of the *quadrivium* (the place where "four roads met"), the four branches of mathematics, which included arithmetic, geometry, astronomy, music was for a long time the privilege of clerics. Number composition impacted upon the development of medieval music, Bernard emphasised mathematics and geometry, mathematics was considered the link between God and world.

Recent studies of a geophysical nature draw attention to natural disasters such as earth tremors or climatological factors. It is known that the earthquake of 1245 destroyed Rathkeltair, Downpatrick and St. Andrew's Abbey and it is hardly likely that the nearby Inch Abbey or Grey Abbey escaped seismic shock waves. Furthermore Ireland is covered with a very thick mantle of boulder clay which in a drought season dries out to such an extent that the foundations of buildings move and vertical cracks develop in walls and may have resulted in roofs sagging, water leaks and perhaps collapse. Indeed foundation problems at Boyle Abbey, County Roscommon called for the walls to be buttressed.

It has been shown that many French Cistercian abbeys have these proportions. In Fontenay, France the ratio of the crossing is 1:1, the ratio of the fifth 2:3, regulates the relation of the width of the crossing to its length, including the choir, and also the relation between the width of the crossing and the total width of nave plus side aisles. Finally, the ratio of the fourth, 3:4 determines the relation between the total width of nave plus side aisles and the length of the transept including chapels.

Elsewhere, I have examined the geology of the sites of Cistercian abbeys in Ireland and the tendency was to place the long axis of the church parallel to the strike of the rocks, to give stability. However, questions such as those relating to water requirements, often led to sloped-sites being chosen. The overall distinctive architectural appearance of Cistercian abbeys with square ends based on the standard plan has been retained in Ireland but it would be difficult from a surveyor's professional examination of these to obtain precise mathematical ratios.

G Carville

Photo 10 -
Carved stones, Baltinglass Abbey

Chapter 5 | Monastic chant and acoustic jars

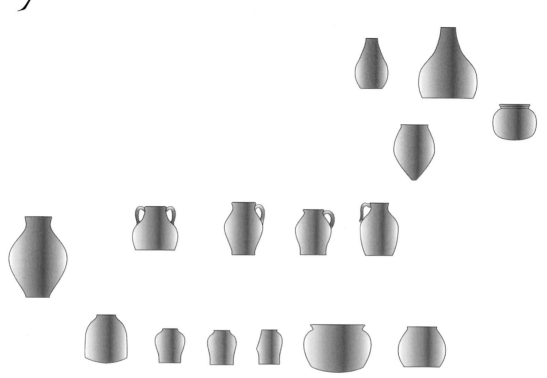

Architecture is amongst St. Bernard's greatest contributions to Medieval Ireland. Even today when we look at the ruinous buildings, one perceives the harmony of design, there are no contradictions. Nevertheless, with the introduction of stone vaulted ceilings to protect the interiors against fire, an adverse effect on the quality of the singing by monks in choir might occur. Vaulted ceilings increased reflections and reduced diffusion, leading to a significant change in acoustic quality, not alone was the reverberation time lengthened, but the focussing effect of the ceilings brought fluctuations in the reverberant sound with a resultant decline in clarity. Sounds appeared to pile on top of one another to produce an effect of surging confusion.[31] To them, this was unacceptable, they wanted clarity and we are reminded of the attention given to chant, when Stephen de Lexington in 1228 carried out a visitation of Irish monasteries and declared that "it is decreed that the rules of the Order in chanting and psalmody shall be followed, according to the writing of Blessed Bernard".[32]

In the medieval period, there is evidence to show that in two monasteries efforts were made to improve the acoustics. In 1854, during excavations being carried out at Fountains Abbey an arrangement was discovered on each side of the processional passage, consisting of two walled spaces in the form of the Roman capital letter L, depressed about two feet below the level of the floor. In that on the south side, nothing was then discovered but firmly embedded on its west and north sides were nine large vases of rude earthenware [see plan].[33] The purpose of placing earthenware pots in the choirs of the churches may be ascertained from a chronicle of the monastery of Metz, written between 1371 and 1469. Under the year 1432, we read as follows:

"In the year aforesaid in the month of August on the Vigil of the Assumption of Our Lady, after that brother Ode le Roy, our prior had returned from the General Chapter above named, he made and ordered to put pots into the choir of the Church, declaring that he had seen (this done) elsewhere in some church and thinking that it would make the singing better, and that it would resound the stronger. And these were forced in one day by as many workmen as sufficed. But I do not know that they sing any better than they did. And it is certain that the walls were greatly torn to pieces and shaken and many who came to us are very much astonished at which is done there. And they have sometimes said that it would be better if they were now outside, declaring that they verily thought the pots had been put there to catch and take in fools."[34]

The idea was introduced to Fountains Abbey, Yorkshire, but Abbot Huby, who brought the idea back from the continent, in answer to inquiries from other monasteries about their suitability, advised:

"Don't tear up your floors for the purpose on any account. We thought it would make our singing better and that it would resound the stronger but after all we cannot say that the sound is any louder, or the singing of the brethren any better than it was before."[35]

Illustration 2 - *Pots or Jars - Detail.*

Front View of West Wall.

Front View of North Wall.

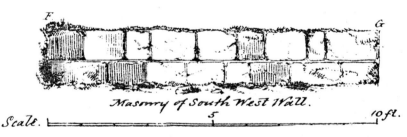

Masonry of South West Wall.

Scale. 5 10 ft.

Illustration to show how these pots or jars were inserted.
AB   *The pots in situ in Fountains Abbey.*
BC   *The masonry slopes upwards towards the east forming an inclined plane.*
FG   *Square holes seem to have been made for the pots and when inserted filled up with rubble.*

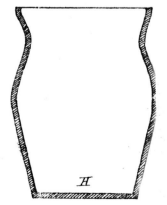

Section of Earthenware Vessel.
Scale. 6 12 in

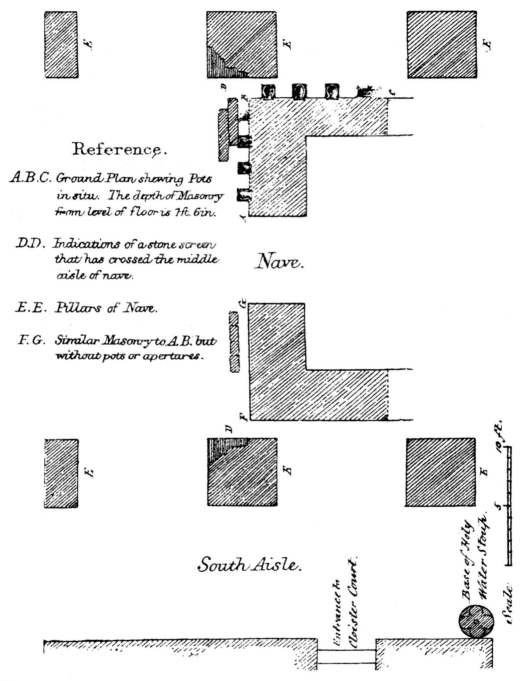

Pots or Jars - Detail.

North Aisle.

Reference.

A.B.C. *Ground Plan shewing Pots in situ. The depth of Masonry from level of floor is 7ft. 6in.*

D.D. *Indications of a stone screen that has crossed the middle aisle of nave.*

E.E. *Pillars of Nave.*

F.G. *Similar Masonry to A.B. but without pots or apertures.*

Nave.

South Aisle.

Entrance to Cloister Court.

Base of Holy Water Stoup.

Scale.

With permission

Illustration to show how these pots or jars were inserted.
AB The pots in situ in Fountains Abbey.
BC The masonry slopes upwards towards the east forming an inclined plane.
FG Square holes seem to have been made for the pots and when inserted filled up with rubble.

In Dunbrody Abbey, Ireland, there is an acoustic chamber consisting of a number of small openings in the upper storey of the tower, in the thickness of the walls [see plan 6].

Plan 6 *Plan of the tower at Dunbrody*

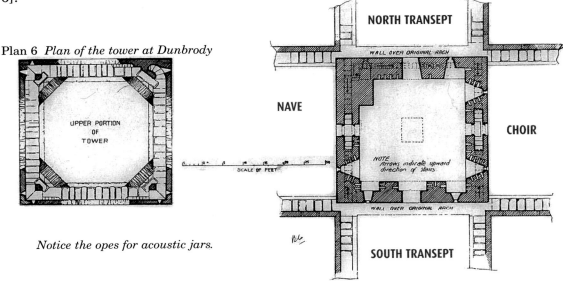

Notice the opes for acoustic jars.

They measure from five inches square in the opening, extending sixteen inches into the wall, the largest is eight inches square and extends twenty-two inches into the wall. There are at least forty on the east wall, twenty five on the west, fifteen on the north and ten on the south. They are arranged around the interiors and in the jambs of the openings.[36]

Photo 10 - *Acoustic apertures in the tower of Dunbrody.*

St. Mary's Church at Youghal, some fifty miles south west of Dunbrody, had similar openings in the choir of the church. These are from three inches to six inches diameter and at a height of twenty-five feet from the ground, and in front of each opening is a perforated stone of about four inches in thickness inside of which are the mouths of earthenware vessels of different shapes and varying in size from eleven inches by seven inches to fifteen and a half inches by eleven and a half inches.[37] The openings of Dunbrody Abbey are in the chamber below the upper or bell stage. Unfortunately these apertures do not contain jars or vases today.

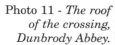

Photo 11 - *The roof of the crossing, Dunbrody Abbey.*

G Carville

G Carville

Photo 12 - *Acoustic apertures in the jambs of the walls of the windows in Dunbrody*

Photo 14 - Acoustic apertures in the tower of Dunbrody

G Carville

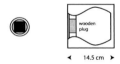

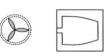

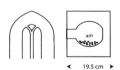

Places within the Church where acoustic jars were sometimes placed.
New Grove Dictionary of Music and Musicians Vol.1

It appears that these pots were used both as absorbers and as resonators and were especially manufactured. Most of them were between 20 cms and 30 cms in length and probably resonated at fundamental frequencies of between 90 and 350 Hz. They were 13 to 15 cms wide at the mouth and the mouths of the wider jars were often reduced in aperture by being placed behind perforated stone or wooden screens or partly plugged with a wooden block, but a number of vases appear never to have had any such constriction of the opening. The former seems to have been intended to act as absorbing resonators to reduce echoes in corners or in the vaults, the latter as resonators to enhance or assist sound.[38] The illustration from Fountains Abbey shows that these jars were made of burnt clay and were often glazed (see photo). They were built on and embedded in mortar in the apertures. Contrary to the experience of Abbot Huby with his under floor arrangement, the vertical wall type were successful. Referring to his own experience of them in St. Mary's, Youghal, Richard Rolt Brash says:

"I can testify to the effect produced by these acoustic jars. I have frequently worshipped in the church and have been many times struck with the fact that when kneeling at the extreme end of the north transept, I could hear most distinctly the communion service though read by a person of very moderate power. The voice appeared to have a peculiarly sonorous and ringing tone."[39]

Photo 14 - Acoustic jar of the type that might have been inserted in the apertures of the tower of Dunbrody. Sometimes rather than baked clay pots, brass ones were used. Fr. Hilary O.C.S.O., Mount Saint Bernard Abbey, England.

G Carville

A further reference to the effectiveness of these jars is contained in a satire by Claude Pithoy, published in 1662 at St. Leger, Luxemburg. He reproved the clergy for negligence of their duties:

> "Of fifty singing men that the public maintain in such a house there are sometimes not more than six present at the service. The choirs are so fitted with jars in the vaults and in the walls that six voices make as much noise as forty elesewhere."[40]

The non-discovery of earthenware jars in Dunbrody, might suggest that brass pots were used and later perhaps sold after the dissolution of the monastery. However there is no mention of the sale of such items in the documents relating to the dissolution of that abbey. It is known that such vessels for acoustic purposes were used by the early Greeks and Italians in their theatres.

> "Still further to increase the resonance of the voice, brazen vases resembling bells were placed in different parts of the theatre. It is well known that when two instruments in harmony are placed within the sphere of each other's influence, if one be struck, the other will vibrate the corresponding chord and the vibration of the second will of course increase and strengthen the sound of the first."[41]

Illustration 3
Section through a Greek theatre showing the direct wavefront of sound reflected from the orchestra floor and the Skene (after Bagenal and Wood).

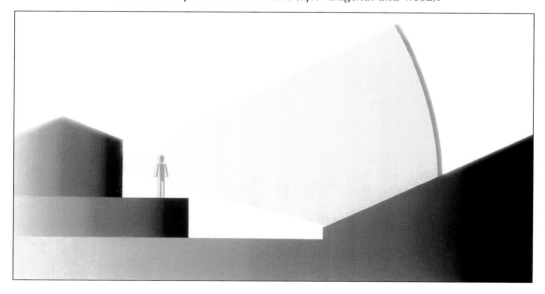

The Greek theatre acted on this principle, which particularly suited the recitative in which dramatic compositions were delivered, the ancients had echeia of earth and metal modulated to the intervals of the different notes of the voice placed in small cells under the seats in one, two or three rows, according to the extent of the theatre. Hence it resulted that the voice, passing from the scene as the centre, expanded itself all round, and striking the cavity of those vases, produced a clearer and more distinct sound by means of the consonance of these different modulated tones, and extended the powers of the speaker to the utmost limits of the cavea.[42]

The wonder of these is explained by Vitruvius in *De architectura* (1st century BC). In Chapter 5 he referred to acoustic vases (echea):

"Now in accordance with these researches, bronze vases should be made in mathematical proportions (to each other) taking into account the size of the theatre and they should be designed so that when they are excited they sound a series of notes at intervals of a fourth, fifth and so on up to two octaves.

Then cubicles should be built among the auditorium seats on the basis of music theory and the vases placed in them in such a way that they are not in contact with any of the upright stonework and have a free space around and above; they should be placed upside down with wedges not less than 15 cms high under them on the side facing the stage. And in line with these cubicles opening should be left [in] the slabs of the lower rows [0.62 m] wide and [0.15 m] deep. The method of marking out the positions in which the jars are to be placed is as follows. If the theatre is not very large, a horizontal line should be marked out halfway up the slope [of the auditorium] and 13 vaulted cubicles built, with 12 equal intervals between them then the sounding jars are placed in them. So by this arrangement, the voice radiating from the stage as from a centre spreads itself around [the auditorium] and by exciting resonance in particular vases, produces an increased clarity and a series of notes which harmonize with itself."[43]

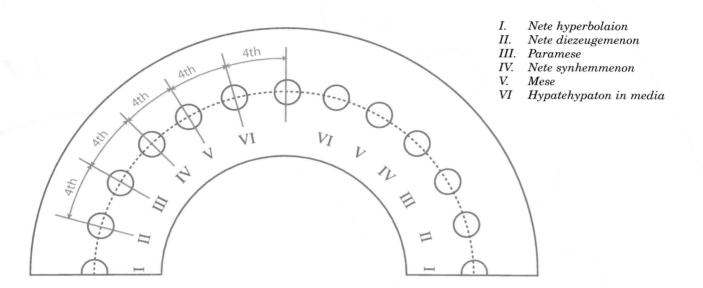

I.   *Nete hyperbolaion*
II.   *Nete diezeugemenon*
III. *Paramese*
IV.   *Nete synhemmenon*
V.   *Mese*
VI   *Hypatehypaton in media*

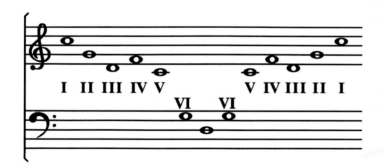

Illustration 5
'Illustration of a Roman theatre according to Vitruvius showing the disposition of acoustic vases he recommended and with pitches (with Greek names) to which they should be tuned (after Landels 1967)'
Groves Musical Dictionary.

The Cistercians wanted clarity. The term for clarity, *claritas* is probably an equivalent for the Greek term *lamproteo*, defined by Aristotle in *De audibilis*, implying, beside distinctness, loudness and purity, and the context almost certainly implies a singing rather than a speaking voice. The function of the vases would have been to make some sounds louder than others, and to make them purer by stressing their fundamentals and suppressing their harmonics or overtones. The series of notes which harmonise with the voice seem to refer to the fact that each vase would resonate and then re-radiate sound after the voice had ceased singing its fundamental note so that if the condordant scale were sung a number of the vases might be heard sounding together, in this way a kind of artificial reverberation time (estimated as 0.2-0.5 seconds) of particular quality would be produced in an open-air theatre, that otherwise had none. Unfortunately no remains of bronze resonators from antiquity have survived.[44]

Little modern research has been done on the effectiveness of such earthenware jars.

Besides Dunbrody and St. Mary's, Youghal, medieval acoustic jars were used widely in Western Europe. Areas of spaced jars in two or three rows inserted in the stone walls of the interior above ground level, usually about 2.5 m from the floor with their mouths opening into the nave or choir may be seen at Fairwell near Lichfield, England. At Leeds Church, near Maidstone, Kent 48-52 vases where extended down the full length of both side walls of the church. Similar jars have been found inserted at regular intervals across the stone barrel vaulting of the choir at St. Martin, Angers, whilst at Bjerelsjoe, Sweden there were about 45 jars in five rows (see map). Acoustic jars were also inserted in the steeper walls below the choir stalls or in pits or cavities as at Fountains in the Church of St. Peter, Mountergate, Norwich, where sixteen jars were placed [see map 7].[45]

Map 7 - *Distribution of Acoustic Jars in Buildings in Medieval Europe*

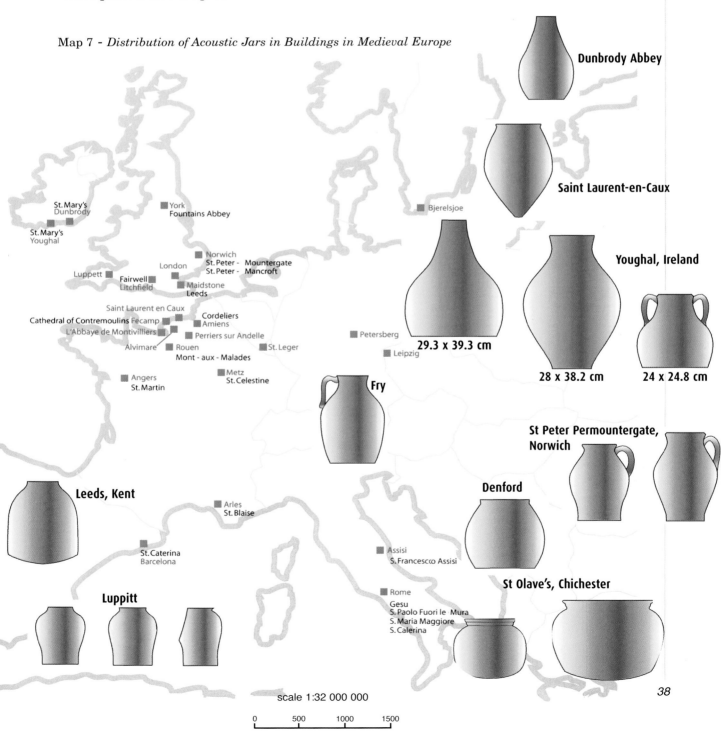

The jars used were either specially made as at Leeds, Kent, where there were 50 jars with their bottoms perforated and Luppett, Devon, which had about six jars flattened on one side. Most of the jars were between 20 cm and 30 cm in length and probably resonated at fundamental frequencies of between 90 and 350 Hz. They were 13-15 cm wide at the mouth, the mouths of the wider jars were often reduced in aperture by being placed behind perforated stone or wooden screens as at Denford, Northamptonshire and St. Mary's Tower, Ipswich, or partly plugged with a wooden block, but a number of vases appear never to have had any such constriction of the opening. The former seems to have been intended to act as absorbing resonators, to reduce echoes in corners or in the vaults, the latter as resonators to enhance or assist sound. The Metz Chronicle (1432) establishes their function clearly: *il fit et ordonnoct de mettre les pots au cuer de l'eglise et pensant qu'il y fesoit milleur chanter e que il ly resonneroit plus fort.*

The presence of acoustic jars are a valuable indication of the attitude of medieval designers to acoustics and their presence in Cistercian monasteries to their singing in the church.

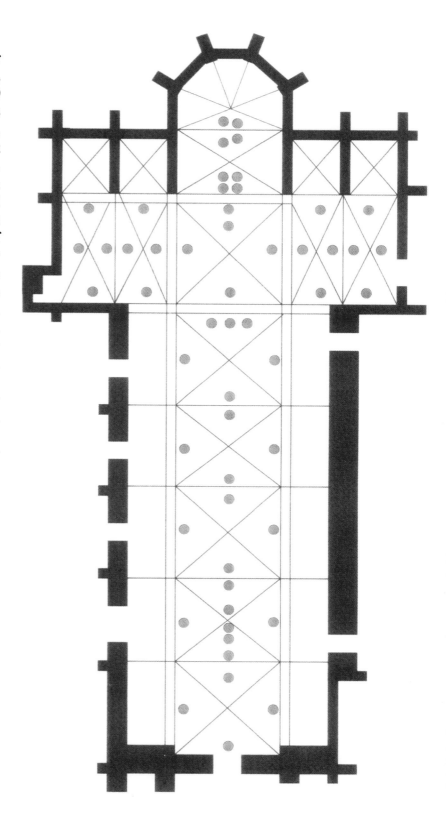

Plan 7 - *The fifty five Vetruvian Jars in the church of Loc-Dieu*
(Taken from Camille De Montelivet, 1997)
By kind permission Konemann Verlagsgesellschaft mbH.

The following is an extract from a letter I received from Fr. Gregory, Mount St. Bernard Abbey, Leicester, England re "Pottery jars in contemporary Cistercian choirs for resonance ..." 20th July 1985.

"I [Fr. Gregory] was present when the old choir stalls were broken up in c.1939 when the extension (*ansliary cepit* of Fr. John Morson's stone plaque over the East Doorway ... entrance to present secular church ...) was finished and we were ready to transfer to it while the old part was altered to its present state. I knew about the pottery jars found under the choir stalls of the ruined Cistercian Abbey of Whalley in Lancashire. So, I looked eagerly for the similar jars under our old high choir stalls. There was merely a deep space under the choir floor boards. The top row was two steps up in contrast to the present one step up. The hollow space made a good sounding board and gave resonance.

Too much resonance for a clumsy Novice! If one dropped a small booklet like 'the Ordo' the sound it made on the hollow floor was enough to count as 'disturbing the choir' ... an offence ... in those days for which one had to pay the automatic penalty of going out and prostrating at the 'presbytery step', the entrance to the 'presbytery' or sanctuary ... which has four steps today.

Fr. Peter Logue who was in Mount St. Bernard Abbey as an interpreter for the Abbatial election in June (accompanying the French Abbot visitor from Melleray, France), said that Dom du Bissey had told him that the acoustic jars in the ancient church at Mt. Melleray (France) had been plastered over ... and have recently been rediscovered and allowed to help the divine office in Choir. The result was striking.

Fr. Logue said that the jars were 'tuned to the note la and that their echoing note helped to bring the choir back to the reciting or singing note' ... Each pottery jar or hollow shape like a glass vase has its own note."
Father Gregory monk of Mt. St. Bernard Abbey, England born 23rd November 1911, died 8th April 1995.

From an Irish perspective when looking at the wide distribution of these jars in Europe the Cistercians in Dunbrody, Ireland, availed of the foremost acoustic technology to make their singing satisfactory in the medieval period.
*Comment: 'tuned to the note **la**' in above letter see the system of Hexachords - chapter 8.*

Chapter 6 | The Cistercians and music - Today as yesterday

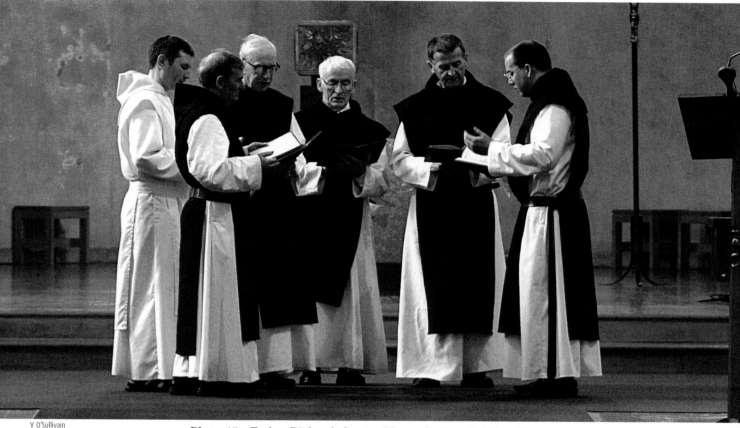

V O'Sullivain

*Photo 15 - Father Richard, Cantor Mount St Joseph Abbey, Roscrea,
with (L-R) Father Liam, Br. Vladimir, Br. Oliver, Br. Dominic and Dom Kevin at choir practice.*

Solus qui cantat audit - Only he who sings hears. The Song of Songs.

St. Benedict's rule underlines the importance of the singing of the liturgy.
*"Let us then consider how we should behave ourselves in the sight of God and his angels and
so sing the psalms that our minds may be in harmony with our voices." Ch.19.*

In the medieval period, the Cistercians aimed to sing all the psalms in seven days and
to do so entered the church seven times a day to sing Matins before daybreak –
*between the day that is passing and the day that is yet to come; they saw the light of
every rising morn* – St. Ambrose; Lauds at sunrise, in Ireland about 4.30 am, Prime at
6 am, Terce at 9 am, Sext at noon, None at 3 pm, Vespers 6 pm, and Compline at 8 pm.
In all it has been estimated that this took four hours.

Religious chant has been studied by the Contemplative Orders since the days of
St. Ambrose and Pope St. Gregory the Great. John the Deacon, who was a secretary to
the latter, says that when he was writing down what the Pope said to him the latter
at times saw a dove (the Holy Spirit) resting on one of the Pope's shoulders,
whispering to him modes and melodies, as though they came from heaven. This was
the chant used in church services.

Through time, the music became lax and lost its Gregorian characteristics. The Cistercians in the twelfth century wanted to return to the chant of this great pope, Gregory the Great. They wanted authentic music. In 790, Charlemagne the Holy Roman Emperor had set up a school of chant at Metz and it was claimed to have preserved the original Gregorian chant. The Cistercians asked for a copy of the so called authentic antiphonary of St. Gregory and it was brought back to Stephen Harding, the third abbot of Citeaux. The latter, even though he had undertaken the revision of the Bible, the Great Bible of Citeaux, did not alter the "Metz text", believing it to be the original and its use in Cistercian abbeys was prescribed for all of them.

By 1134, the Cistercians were not happy with the chant and when Abbot Stephen Harding died in 1134, the General Chapter declared that "the irregularities were untenable and marred the Cistercian choral books". The Metz manuscript seemed to have been changed both in text and music. Bernard of Clairvaux had a recognised reputation for music. He was a composer who had been invited by an abbot of another monastery, to compose an office for the Feast of St. Victor. He said that what he demands of ecclesiastical music, is that "it radiate truth and that it sound the great Christian virtues". Music should please the ear in order to move the heart, it should be striking a golden mean between the frivolous and the harsh, wholesomely affect man's entire nature. For him heavenly bliss in music is an eternal listening to and participating the choirs of angels and saints.

The General Chapter wanted Bernard to undertake the revision of the "Metz" text but he was so involved with the Anaclectus schism that he had no time available to undertake the work and he gave it to one of his former novices, Guy, who was now Abbot of Cherlieu (1132-57) one of his daughter houses, and his secretary William, who later became Abbot of Rievaulx, England. Guy of Cherlieu says that when he was a novice, Bernard often discussed chant with him.

Sarah Fuller in the Catholic Encyclopedia (527) has drawn attention to a problem of identification of Cistercian manuscripts in the Middle Ages, with a single author rather than with two individuals. She points out that the preface to the Cistercian Gradual, *Prefatio seu tractus de cantu* in the eighteenth and nineteenth century, was attributed to Guido of Cherlieu. However these manuscripts have now disappeared and it is impossible to examine this statement. Furthermore another work *Regule de arte musica*, is believed to be the work of a Cistercian theorist, Guido of Eu.

The mid-12th century Cistercian *Tonale Sancti Bernardi* advises anyone seeking more information on certain theoretical topics to consult "the book of music that Guido of Eu wrote for his mentor Guillaume (William), Abbot of Rievaulx". This probably means that as his mentor they both lived in the same abbey, namely Clairvaux (as did Guy who later became Abbot of Cherlieu).

There is also a 13th century catalogue of Richart de Fournival's library which credits a thirteenth century treatise to Guido of Eu as well. This may be *Regule de arte musica* (in F-Psg 2284) attributed in its explicit (at the end) to an Abbot Guido (*'Expliciunt regule domni Guidonis abbatis de arte musica'*).

However the *Regule* is addressed to a distinguished cleric, a master of the novices at Clairvaux, who had encouraged the author's chant studies, in other words this 'author' was a monk of Bernard's community and the distinguished cleric, the foremost scholar of the day being Bernard. Sweeney, C. in Johannis Wylde *Musica Manualis Cum Tonale*, CSM, XXVIII (1982, p.90) has shown that the connection between Guido of Eu and the *Regule* is further strengthened by a 15th century English treatise that quotes extensively from the *Regule* and credits that material to Guido of Eu and concludes that there is strong circumstantial evidence to link the music theorist Guido of Eu named in the Cistercian tonary *Tonale Sancti Bernardi* with the Abbot Guido (of Cherlieu) named in the explicit to the *Regule de arte musica*, in its sole surviving source. There is another very important document, the Preface to the Cistercian Gradual *Prefatio seu tractus de cantu*, which includes doctrines of the *Regule*, with the result that scholars of the seventeenth and nineteenth centuries assigned it to Abbot Guido of Cherlieu, who was abbot there from 1132 to 1157. For my part, Guido of Eu and Guido of Cherlieu are the same person. As a member of Bernard's community before 1132, "Eu" may indicate the district from which he came, but he was already made Abbot of Cherlieu before the General Chapter in 1135 took the decision to have the chant reviewed and revised. He may have had the *Regule* commenced in 1130 finished, while in Clairvaux and then worked on the *Gradual* after he moved to the Abbey of Cherlieu. This would help to explain why the doctrines of the *Regule* are contained in the Preface to the Cistercian *Gradual*.

The Cistercian tradition has been one of anonymity, seldom can one find for example a complete succession list of abbots, the attitude was that it was the office held and how that office was carried out that was important, thus we have office holders such as the prior, the procurator, the porter, the grange master rather than named individuals.

In the *Regule de arte musica* and the discant treatise, the *Regule* concentrates on plain chant theory. This was not new, about one hundred years before this Guido of Arezzo (b c.991-2; d after 1033) developed a system of precise pitch notation, through four lines and spaces, and promoted a method of sight singing which relied on the syllables ut, re, me, fa, sol, la. He produced two works, the *Micrologus*, a comprehensive treatise on musical practice and included in it a discussion of both polyphonic music and plain chant. In his *Prologus* and in the *Regulae rhythmicae* which are intended as guides to the use of the antiphoner he includes the new notation and begins with the gamut of twenty one notes:

ΓABCDEFG ab♭cdefg

ab♭cd

ab♭cd

the tetrachords, a scale of four notes embracing the interval of a perfect fourth, intervals, namely the pitch difference between two notes, expressed in terms of the diatonic scale, for example a fifth or as a harmonic ratio 3:2. Guido de Cherlieu, accepts all seven pitches as finals, and limits the ambitus of any chant to ten pitches and this provided the foundation for an extensive revision of the Cistercian chant repertory asked for by the General Chapter 1135. There is also a brief discant treatise that puts forward rules for the movement of two voices from one perfect consonance to another.

Photo 16 - Psalms and Canticles

Photo 17 - Choir practice

Chapter 7 | CANTOR - Sub-Cantor and Assistant Cantors

V O'Sullivain

Photo 18 - Vespers, Mount St. Joseph Abbey

The study and cultivation of music was looked upon with favour in Cistercian monasteries. It can be said that the Liturgy of the Hours, the prayer of the monks was given proper expression. The founders of the Order were determined to have a common liturgy. It was required that all monasteries have the usages and chant and all the books needed for the day and night hours and for Mass according to the form of the usage and books of the "New Monastery" – Citeaux. The early Cistercians were concerned with authenticity and for this a liturgy which was marked by simplicity was necessary, particularly regarding the chant, and the monk known as a Cantor was appointed. He had a Sub-Cantor and Assistant Cantors to help him.

The Cantor

"The Cantor is placed in the choir, on the side of the Abbot, about mid-way. The Cantor, with the agreement of the Abbot, regulates the tone and the pace of the singing. Therefore the choir must be told in advance how that office is to be sung. He sees that the rules of the chant are strictly observed and if any monk departs from the rules, he draws his attention to the problem by means of tablets (see photo) – he never vocally corrects during the service. If a monk mistakes one verse for another, he waits until he has finished and then corrects his mistake. When a psalm has been intoned too high or too low, the Cantor on the side where it was intoned lowers or raises the tone at the mediant. If the Cantor is not a priest, the Sub-Cantor, if he is a priest, corrects the faults of the Hebdomadary (the monk who made the mistake) otherwise it is left to the Father Sub-Prior. An official who has omitted to correct a fault goes to prostrate with the one who committed it.

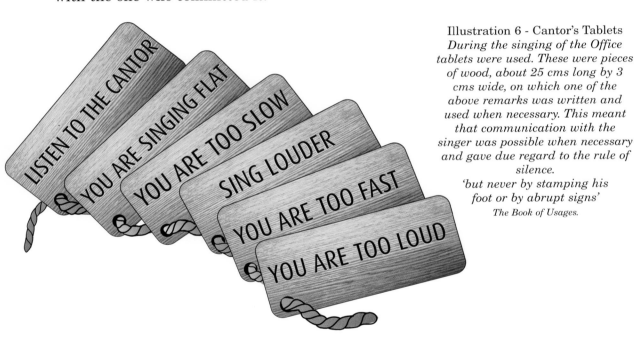

Illustration 6 - Cantor's Tablets
During the singing of the Office tablets were used. These were pieces of wood, about 25 cms long by 3 cms wide, on which one of the above remarks was written and used when necessary. This meant that communication with the singer was possible when necessary and gave due regard to the rule of silence.
'but never by stamping his foot or by abrupt signs'
The Book of Usages.

The Cantor intones all the antiphons, at the end of the psalm and the common commemorations. The psalms without the antiphon are taken up by the whole side on which they fall. The Cantor's duty is to intone the hymns of the Canonical Office on days of twelve lessons and during the Octaves of Christmas, Easter and Pentecost except at Sext and None. Along with the Sub-Cantor he has to make the responsories at vespers. During Octaves (except those of Christmas, Easter and Pentecost) on days of three lessons and on ferial days, he intones the *Benedictus* and *Magnificat* antiphons. On other days, during the hymn or the versicle, he announces the antiphon to the Abbot, and he intones the canticle. If the Abbot is absent the Cantor intones the antiphon. When the responsories are sung, he takes to the novices bookstand for the night office, the board on which are marked those who are to sing the lessons and responsories. During the twelfth lesson, the Cantor goes to the Abbot and invites him by a bow to come and sing the last responsary at the stand.

M McKernon

Today as yesterday .....

If the Mass is sung by the priest alone, the Cantor appoints the cleric who is to sing the Epistle. If all the clerics are not able to sing the Prophecies on Ember Days, he appoints on the previous day, those who are to sing them. The Cantor and Sub-Cantor present themselves after the novices, to receive the candles, ashes and palms and to perform the adoration of the cross. At the last station, the Cantor tells the Abbot the antiphon of Solemn Processions, at the moment when the community are about to enter the church. When the Abbot says any public prayer, without being accompanied by a priest, the Cantor holds the book open before him.

Every Friday, the Cantor arranges the tablet of the officers; he then presents it to the Superior. The officers are appointed in the following order; *Invitatorium, Missam Majorem, Missam de Beata, Missam pro defunctes, Evangelium, Epistolam, Servitor ecclesiae, Lector mensae servitor coquinae*. He only appoints those who are able to do these duties, with edification. Novices and servants of the refectory are not appointed. The Cantor chooses for Deacon and Sub-Deacon those who are able to fulfil the duty, whether professed novices or oblates.

It is the Cantor's duty to regulate the Latin lecture in the refectory and to point out to the reader the place in the Bible at which he is to begin. If the book of the Bible has not been finished in the time appointed for reading it, he makes a note of it in order that it may be resumed at the same place, the following year. He also sees to it that the Constitutions are read. When the reader in the refectory cannot be present at the end of Mass to sing *Domine labie* etc., the Cantor takes his place. He receives the blessing for those serving in the refectory, if the Cellarer is absent.

The books for the processions and *Mandatum* are confided to his care. He has to see to it that the choir books are in good condition and if any of them needs to be repaired he has to inform the Abbot. No change can be made either in the words or notes, without the Abbot's permission.

The Cantor gives the singing lesson to the novices, which is held three times a week, and lasts about half an hour; in summer, it can be given during work time. The teacher can tell the novices at the class as to what concerns him, but the novices do not reply. He also gives the singing lesson to the professed monks, when the Abbot thinks it necessary. On the first Sunday of Advent, he reads in Chapter the Statute on Detraction.

Photo 20 - The Gothic method of vaulting gave a high light-filled sanctuary. Covered ceilings with small ribs or coffering reduced the fluctuations of sound by increasing uniform diffusion.

On the first Sunday of Lent, during the early morning Mass, the Matutinal Mass, the Cantor and a few monks appointed by the Prior, brings from the library to the Chapter, the books chosen beforehand and places them in order on a table, in front of the Abbot's seat. After the Holy Rule is explained, the distribution of books takes place. When the Cantor reaches the table on which are the books, he first bows to the Crucifix, then takes the book for the Abbot and gives it to him with both hands, bowing before and after. The Sub-Cantor does the same with the Prior, then each of them accompanied by his Assistant Cantor, hands the books one by one to the monks. On Friday in Passion week, the Cantor puts out a tablet on which he marks those who are to sing the *Gloria Laus*, and the Passion.

On Easter Sunday, after the community have entered Chapter and before the reading of the Martyrology, the Cantor announces the Paschal Solemnity at the desk. He does not read the Martyrology but returns to his place. Every Saturday in Ember week, following the first Sunday in Lent, Whitsunday, Holy Cross and St. Lucia's Day, he reads in Chapter the last Visitation Card and the Definitions of the last General Chapter.

If Holy Viaticum is to be given after Extreme Unction, the Cantor carries the Blessed Sacrament to the sick. After the ceremony, he returns to the sacristy, behind the Abbot and carrying the empty *ciborium*.

When the death is announced the Cantor takes to the infirmary a Ritual for the Superior and processionals for the religious. He distributes candles given to him by the sacristan to the novices or junior professed. After the body has been placed in the Church, he appoints two religious to remain and recite the psalter and then immediately appoints two monks to remain, and then prepares a tablet which he gets approved by the Abbot and in which he assigns to each a half hour to watch the body.

If there is a deceased person, and a death notice to be read, the Cantor does it in Chapter. After the explanation of the Holy Rule when the Abbot has said *Loquamur de Ordine nostro*, the Cantor comes forward into the middle, bows and says: *Absolvatis animam fraters n defuncti;* or *Absolvats patrem, pratris nostril n paper deufnctum* or *Hodel finilier tricenarium fratris "n"* adding his quality of priest; or he reads the death notice which has been received; he then bows again and returns to his place. The death notices are read at the first Chapter after they are received then he puts them in the cloister or other place appointed for the purpose and removes them eight days afterwards.

The Sub-Cantor

The Sub-Cantor is placed on the left side in choir, about the middle. He never goes to the other side when the Cantor is present, but he corrects those on his own side when they make mistakes, as laid down in the preceding Chapter, which he should consult. He intones the hymns on his own side, like the Cantor. On Feasts of Sermon he sings the solemn Responsory at Vespers and the twelfth at Matins at the stand with the Cantor. If the Cantor is absent or unable to fulfil his duties, the Sub-Cantor supplies for him in everything, except in the cases mentioned in these Regulations. When he intones, in place of the Cantor, anything which is sung in two choirs, the religious on the Abbot's side continue it. When the Cantor is Hebdomadary, the Sub-Cantor intones the Commemorations at Lauds and Vespers, and the antiphon *Spiritus Sanctus* at all the Offices, as also the psalm *Laudate* at the Grace after supper on days of two meals, the psalm *De profundis* at the Grace after dinner, and the *Benedicite* at collation.

Assistant Cantors

The Assistant Cantors are placed below the Cantors. In the absence of the first Cantor, it is the Assistant Cantor of the same side who announces the *Benedictus* and *Magnificat* antiphons to the Reverend Father Abbot, and then intones the canticle. When either of the Cantors is absent, the Assistant Cantor of the same side supplies for him in intoning the hymns, etc. If they are both absent, the Assistant Cantors supply for them in everything. If the latter are themselves absent, the religious placed immediately above supply for them."[46]

DIE XXIV. JUNII

In Nativitate S. Joannis Baptistae

AD VESPERAS

Hymnus.

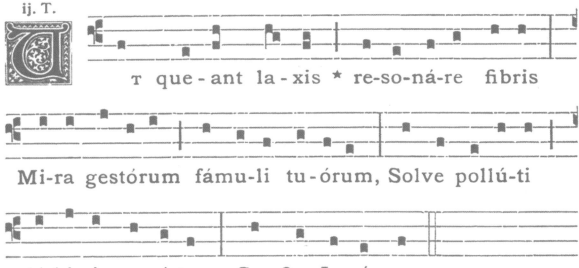

ij. T.

UT que-ant la-xis * re-so-ná-re fibris

Mi-ra gestórum fámu-li tu-órum, Solve pollú-ti

lá-bi-i re-á-tum, Sancte Jo-ánnes.

Our Lady of Bolton Abbey, Moone

Chapter 8 | Psalter 36929

Photo 22 - Psalterium Davidicum, M. DCCC. LV. ad usum Sacri Ordinis Cisterciensis, Per Hebdomadam Dispositum.

Psalter 36929 was written (transcribed) by a Cistercian monk called Cormac in the thirteenth century. It has already been mentioned that Stephen Harding (St.), second Abbot of Citeaux undertook a revision of the Bible, the "Great Bible of Citeaux", now in the museum of Dijon, and when doing so he sought and received help from expert and learned rabbis in the Troyes area of France. This manuscript still retains all the corrections that were made to it, thus Psalm 151 was accepted by the Cistercians at that time as a continuation of Psalm 150. Furthermore (see Chapter 2) the mother house had to provide all the books for the Divine Office for a daughter house. These in the case of the first foundations, such as Mellifont Abbey and Baltinglass Abbey would have been brought from Clairvaux Abbey, France.

Cormac was and is a popular name in Ireland, and is found in place names such as Cormackstown, Kilcormack, Killeen Cormac. The Cistercians in thirteenth century Ireland, were not dependent upon fragments of a seventh century manuscript of another Cormac in writing psalter 36929. Furthermore the music is medieval organum.

This manuscript has a colophon with words and music by Cormac, which illustrates the theoretical and practical knowledge of Cistercian monks in the thirteenth century. In Chapter 4 it has been shown that the ratio of the chords were reflected in the layout of the abbey church based on a plan from Villard de Honnecourt's notebook, a church for the Order of Citeaux, which gave perfect symmetry or harmony in the architectural plan and in Chapter 5 a description was given of church walls, with small openings for acoustic jars made, to reduce or amplify the sound at intervals of a fourth, within the compass of two octaves.

In this manuscript, transcribed by a Cistercian monk, the musical notation is in the form of modes, neumes and harmony. The old scales used were called modes, "church modes", because the early melody of the church as quoted above and for example in the music of Assaroe medieval Cistercian Abbey was written in modes. The mode depended as to where the semitone occurred that is where B-C or E-F fell (mi-fah). The tonic of the mode, is called the final, and the pitch of a mode could be changed by starting on a different note, so long as the order of tones and semitones stayed the same. The modes are as follows:

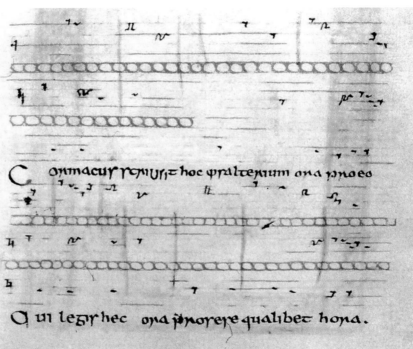

Illustration 7
Polyphony
Manuscript 36929

[odd numbers (Authentic) even numbers (derived) Plagal]						
Dorian	DD (authentic)	Mode I	A(Plagal)	semitones fall	2-3 EF	6-7 BC
Phrygian	EE	III	B		1-2 EF	5-6 BC
Lydian	FF	V	C		4-5 BC	7-8 EF
Mixolydian	GG	VII	D		3-4 BC	6-7 EF
Aeolian	AA		E		2-3 BC	5-6 EF
Ionian	CC				3-4 EF	7-8 BC

This music shows the movable doh clef, which is the tonic or keynote in the tonic sol-fa system which shifts the tonal centre, at each modulation into another key. Present day music would do this by using accidentals of sharps or flats not included in the key signature, or contradicting those in the key signature by use of naturals. The evidence from this passage shows that the Cistercians were sight reading from notation and not just depending on memorizing six tones. Novices were taught to do so and this was an innovation attributed to Guido of Arezzo, an eleventh century monk. The six tones were C D E F G A, the semitone falling between E-F in other words "mi-fah" and to this was set the words of a Hymn to St. John. It became known as solmization, the designation of the musical scales by means of syllables.

Photo 23 - Studying the psalms

V O'Sullivain

Ut/re/mi/fa/so/la
Ut que ant la-xis
C D F D E D
Ut que ant la-xis
D D C D E E
Re so na re fi bris
E G E D E C D
Mi rages to-rum
F G A G F D D
Fa-mu-li-tu-o-rum
G A G E F G D
Sol-ve-po-lu-ti
A G A F G A A
La-bi-i re-a-tum
G F D C E D
Sanc-te Jo-han-nes

Each phrase can serve as an aid to a singer wishing to read a particular melody. Guido lived over one hundred years before the advent of the Cistercians and this method was well known and used in church music in Europe.

Another innovation of the ninth century was a form of musical notation called neumes (meaning signs). These were strokes placed over syllables to indicate an ascending note (/) or descending (\) or a combination of the two (/\). Eventually scribes placed neumes at different heights above the syllables of the words to indicate the shape of the melody and these were called "heightened" neumes. Then a red line to represent the pitch was drawn and the neumes were grouped about this line, in time a second line was introduced, coloured yellow and this was for C. This further developed and by the eleventh century Guido of Arezzo described the 4 line staff as in this manuscript passage (36929). The monks could now sight read the precise and relative pitch of the notes, they were free from having to depend on memorising the chant.

Regarding note values, when this passage was composed and transcribed time signatures had not been introduced. The practice was to treat the notes of a chant as if they all had the same basic value. This type of music was called plain chant or plain song and there were four styles of word setting associated with it, namely syllabic, one note of the melody to one syllable; neumatic, two to four notes to one syllable; psalmodic, several notes to one syllable (as in the music of Assaroe) and melismatic; many notes with a flowing and wave like melody to one syllable, as in this abstract; there were however no bar lines, no 'measured' time.

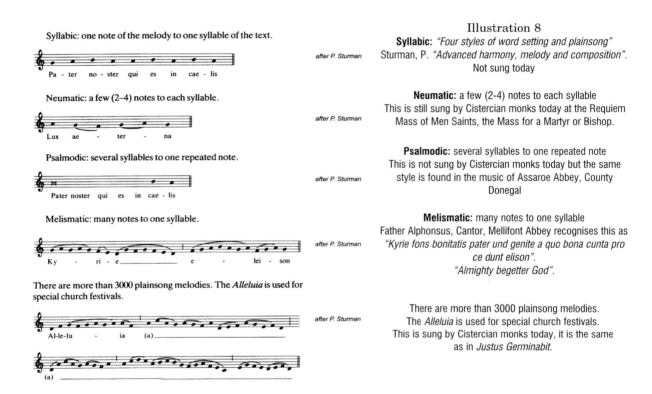

Syllabic: one note of the melody to one syllable of the text.

Pa - ter no - ster qui es in cae - lis

after P. Sturman

Neumatic: a few (2–4) notes to each syllable.

Lux ae - ter - na

after P. Sturman

Psalmodic: several syllables to one repeated note.

Pater noster qui es in cae - lis

after P. Sturman

Melismatic: many notes to one syllable.

Ky - ri - e _____ e - lei - son

after P. Sturman

There are more than 3000 plainsong melodies. The *Alleluia* is used for special church festivals.

Al-le-lu - ia (a) _____

after P. Sturman

(a) _____

Illustration 8
Syllabic: *"Four styles of word setting and plainsong"* Sturman, P. *"Advanced harmony, melody and composition"*. Not sung today

Neumatic: a few (2-4) notes to each syllable This is still sung by Cistercian monks today at the Requiem Mass of Men Saints, the Mass for a Martyr or Bishop.

Psalmodic: several syllables to one repeated note This is not sung by Cistercian monks today but the same style is found in the music of Assaroe Abbey, County Donegal

Melismatic: many notes to one syllable Father Alphonsus, Cantor, Mellifont Abbey recognises this as *"Kyrie fons bonitatis pater und genite a quo bona cunta pro ce dunt elison"*. *"Almighty begetter God"*.

There are more than 3000 plainsong melodies. The *Alleluia* is used for special church festivals. This is sung by Cistercian monks today, it is the same as in *Justus Germinabit*.

This type of music is known as *organum* which in early medieval harmony was one in which voices moved in parallel fourths or fifths, thus the idea of two distinct voices caught on. Guido d'Arezzo allowed a modified form of parallel *organum*, he rejected the interval of the fifth, and the minor second, the perfect fourth, and major and minor thirds and major second. He wanted *occursus*, that was the coming together of two voices on a unison at the end of a phrase. A third progressing by contrary motion to a unison must be a major, as must also be a second that proceeds to a unison by oblique motion, to avoid semitone cadences in plain chant.[47] He accepted the crossing of the principal and the organal voice and more than one note against a single syllable. If the organal voice reached the final before the principal voice, then to avoid parallel motion the organal voice held that note, giving a sort of drone. This passage with moving doh clefs, the four line staff, the three voices shows how advanced this *organum* had become when transcribed in MS 36929. This is *florid organum* or melismatic organum, associated with St. Martial (Limoge) and Notre Dame (Paris).

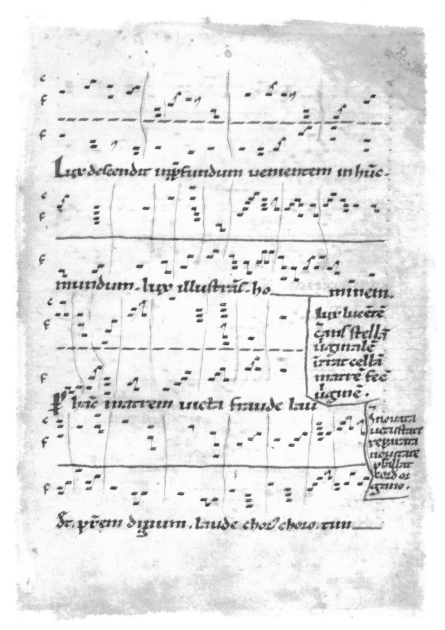

The term *florid organum* was first applied in a two voice texture, *organum duplum vel purum*. By extension it came to be used as a general term to denote all polyphonic music based on Gregorian chant in the middle of the thirteenth century, this however, written by Cormac is *Triplum organum*.

This passage has been transposed by Fr Richard, Mount St. Joseph Abbey, Roscrea and I have a recording of him singing it. I also have a recording of Brother Finbar, Our Lady of Bethlehem Abbey, Portglenone singing the same passage, without transposition and it is easily recognisable as Gregorian chant. Since the rhythmic interpretation of the original notation is not certain, the points at which the voices came together may not be what is shown in Fr Richard's transposition. The monk scribe Cormac has drawn red vertical lines, to relate the neumes to the syllables which is similar to those recorded on a page from a St. Martial manuscript showing the organum *Lux descendit* now in the British Museum.

Correct alignment is difficult to determine, and personal interpretations are not and cannot be described as definitive, but follows the alignment as closely as possible.

The System of Hexachords

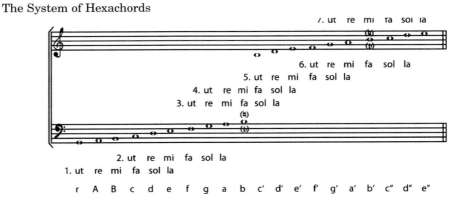

Illustration 10
A hexachord is not a chord in the true sense but a group of six individual notes. Introduced in the eleventh century, as a method of sight - singing; a series of overlapping scalar hexachords embraced the entire compass of notes.

Kyrie: Cunctipotens Genitor Deus

Illustration 11
Folio 65v from the Ordinal of Rosglas which shows that the hexachord was known in that abbey.
This Ordinal ms (11898) was made by a monk in Mellifont Abbey fd1142 (Fons Mellis) for the abbot of Rosglas [see also page 61]. Note semitone between B and C (semitone mi-fa)

An Ordinal indicates an order of sequence: a book of rules: a service book: a book of forms of consecration and ordination.

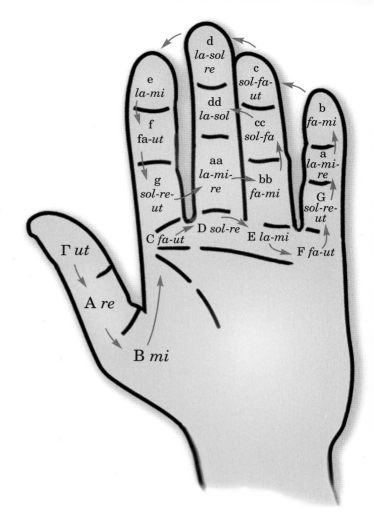

The Guidonian Hand
Att. to Guido of Arezzo

THE GUIDONIAN HAND

How would the Cantor monk have used this hexachord for sight reading? The notes of the gamut were mentally superimposed onto the joints and tips of the left hand then he would have pointed to these with the index finger of his right hand as shown.

"Gamma *ut*" (two Gs below middle C) was the tip of the thumb, A ("A *re*") was the inside of the thumb knuckle, B ("B *mi*") was the joint at the base of the thumb, C ("C *fa ut*") was the joint at the base of the index finger, and so on, moving in an anticlockwise direction past middle C ("C *sol fa ut*") until the D a ninth above middle C ("D *la sol*") (the middle joint of the middle finger) and the E above that ("E *la*") (the back of that joint, the only note on the back of the hand) were reached.

This allowed people to see where the half steps of the gamut were, and to visualise the interlocking positions of the hexachords.

Photo 24 -
*Boyle Abbey
Co. Roscommon*

Duchas

57

Photo 25 - *Jerpoint Abbey, Co. Kilkenny*

Dextera Dei - The hand of God
The magicians said to Pharoah *This is the finger of God.* Exodus 8:19

God
(the hand in
the cloud).

This inset picture was drawn by an English monk in the 13th century. In it, God (the hand in the cloud) is telling St. Bernard what to write. It might appear that Cormac the 13th century Irish scribe of the manuscript 36929 left this folio unfinished. However the same idea is expressed, Cormac the Irish scribe of this psalter is depicted as being instructed by God (the hand in the cloud).

It would be most unlikely that Cormac would have included a drawing of himself, therefore he left the folio blank, but a similar idea is expressed.

A thirteenth century pen and ink drawing of St. Bernard writing, inspired by the hand of God. (English Manuscript 13th Century) [*see top right hand corner of this inset*].

'Knowledge that comes from the school of the Holy Spirit rather than the schools of rhetoric will savour all the sweeter to me' *St. Bernard*

Every monastery had a scriptorium

Cistercian monks entered the church seven times a day and in the medieval period, completed the singing of the psalter in a week. For this and the study of the scriptures they needed books, for the business of the monastery they needed to record charters, deeds, wills, details of land transactions, along with letter writing. The abbot's legal adviser was the notary whilst the writing and copying was the work of the monk scribe. To provide for the choir monks, a vast number of manuscripts and books were required and had to be copied. In those days the monks did not write on paper, but on animal skins, which had to be treated and prepared. Vellum was obtained and was a fine kind of parchment, prepared by lime baths and burnishing, from the skins of calves, kids or lambs, whilst parchment was made from the skin of a sheep or goat.

The first three days of November were known as 'blood days', when many young animals were slaughtered, because of a shortage of winter feed. There were other demands too, for skins such as leather for shoes, belts, harnesses and reins, required by those monks and brothers working on the home farm and granges. It has been conservatively estimated that over two hundred skins were needed for the Book of Lindisfarne and how many might we guess for Manuscript 36929, a Psalter in Latin, of St. Jerome's second (or Gallican) version, also written on vellum?

After the skins were dried then they were de-haired and made smooth and clean of all fine animal hair by rubbing with a pumice stone. Writing was done with a stylus or quill and if a mistake was made then a pumice stone was used to erase it. The parchment was ruled, using lead or perhaps graphite with equal spacing giving in MS36929 twenty-two lines in single columns, whilst the number of words varied in each line. The script is in later Irish Insular Maniscule with a formal rounded aspect perhaps influenced by European Romanesque textualis hands. The quill was most likely that of a small bird, the letters are not joined up, so that each time the monk scribe made a letter stroke, he had to raise his wrist.

The work in the *scriptorium* consisted of writing, illumination and binding and might be described as an artistic enterprise. Initials of verses stand in the margin and are filled with patches of colour, chiefly red and yellow; many of them terminate in the heads and claws of dogs and several are outlined with red dots. The initials of psalms are larger, and more elaborate, with interlaced and other designs and similar zoomorphic extremities, the colours used being red, yellow, purple, green and blue. The still larger initials are composed of the elongated bodies of dogs, mostly purple in colour, they are surrounded by a close network of interlaced yellow cords laid on a red ground and terminating in human as well as canine heads.

Such illumination would not have been approved of by St. Bernard, and Statute 82 was issued in 1135 forbidding it. However even the Great Bible of Citeaux has some zoomorphs. A large illuminated letter indicates the first letter of a psalm and was in fact a visual mnemonic for easy recognition whilst a smaller coloured letter marks the beginning of each verse.

In all there are 150 psalms, and are divided after Psalm L (50) and Psalm C (100). On the pages facing Psalm LI (51) and Psalm CI (101) are rectangular frames of interlaced key-pattern and other designs in red, yellow and purple, and may have been intended for miniatures.

The lettering in MS36929 is beautiful, accurate, legible, all the letter strokes are of the same thickness. This must have required complete concentration, however if the monk scribe's attention wandered and he did not concentrate, then he was put on a diet of bread and water. If he did not keep the parchment clean, he was given one hundred and thirty penances, and if he broke his quill in a fit of temper, he was given thirty penances. Natural dyes were obtained from oak apples, red from madder, yellow from the root of saffron, whilst black was obtained from the roe of certain fish. In the twelfth century, Alexander Neckham described how he thought a scribe should be equipped:

> Let him have a razor knife for scraping pages of parchment or skin, let him have a pumice for cleaning the sheets and a little scraper for making equal the surface of the skin. He should have a piece of lead and ruler with which he may rule the margins on both sides … There should be a fold of four sheets … Let these leaves be held together at top and bottom by a strip … Let him sit in a chair with both arms high reinforcing the back rest and with a stool at his feet. There should be hot coals in the heating container, so that the ink may dry more quickly on the parchment in foggy or wet weather … There should be red lead for forming red … letters or capital. Let there be dark powder and blue …

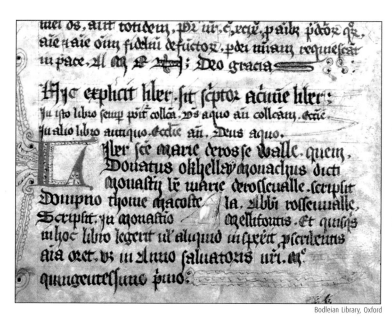

Illustration 11
Folio 67v from the Ordinal of Rosglas.

Liber sancte Marie de Rosse Walle, quem Donatus Okhelly, monachus dicti monasterii beate Marie de Rossevalle scripsit Dompno Thame Macostela, abbati Rossewalle. Scripsit in monasterio Mellifontis et quisquis in hoc libro legerit vel aliquid inspexerit pro scribentis anima oret, viz. in anno salvatoris nostri M°quingentesimo primo.
Iste liber constat monasterii beate Marie Evveyn et omnibus monachis ibeden existentibus. Anno Domini 1509 creatus fuit Donatus Okehellay in priorem per conventum de Rossiavale.
(Catalogue)

An Ordinal indicates an order of sequence: a book of rules: a service book: a book of forms of consecration and ordination.

Illustration 12
Psalm 15
*Notice the
insertion added
in red letters by a
later hand.*

Guard me, O Lord, for in Thee I put my trust!
I say to the Lord: My God art Thou!
For Thou has no need of my possessions.

The importance of the *scriptorium* was stressed even in the seventh century. Cassiodorus favoured the copyists in the *scriptorium* and said "of all the works that can be accomplished by manual labour, none pleases me so much as a copyist, if only they will copy correctly". He compiled a treatise on orthography, the art of practice of spelling words correctly, from the precepts of the grammarians and commended it to the *antiquarri*. He provided a sundial, a water clock, and self trimming oil, supplying lamps to assist them in their work of copying. He also encouraged bookbinding. When a manuscript was finished it was given to the bookbinder who had a large selection of patterns "that a man of taste may choose the form of covering which pleases him best".[48]

British Library

Blessing of Bernard. Prayer before the psalms.

Manuscript 36929 is a Psalter in Latin of St. Jerome's Gallican version, unfortunately the first folio and two at the end are missing. From the Psalter, this is the blessing of St. Bernard:

Which translated (loosely) reads as follows:

> "A blessing of Bernard, and of the blessed Peter, Prince of the Apostles, thro (faculties) granted to us (ie the power of binding and loosing) in as far as your accusation is expedient and is our concern the remission (that is to say) Omnipotent God, Your Redeemer, life, grace and the pious (indultor) (ie forgiver) forever of all your sins."

This is followed by a prayer "Before the Psalms", "Let us pray"

> Deign to accept O Lord, those little consecrated verses, which I a sinner desire to sing in honour of you Our Lord Jesus Christ, my crimes, whether in deeds, or words or thoughts, covetousness, lust, concupiscence, iniquities, or all my negligencies both great and small these go forward to the help of them and the remission of all sins and a space for abjuring and of doing your penance.

Comments of St. Augustine on Psalmis
Expositio St. Augustini Psalmis

It has already been said that St. Bernard was greatly influenced by the works of St. Augustine [350-430], both in his theological formation and number mysticism. The latter wrote over two thousand pages, in four volumes on the one hundred and fifty psalms. Sometimes he made two or three full commentaries on one psalm. This manuscript is not taken from the work of St. Augustine, but from Alcuin (died c.800), who on an Irish chronological scale would have been a contemporary of Aengus Culdee (died c.824). In 792 Alcuin wrote an *Opusculum* titled *De Psalmorum Usu* and this manuscript folio *Exposito St. Augustini Psalmis* is found in it.

Opusculum secundum
De psalmorum usu Liber
Cum variis forumulis ad res
Quotidianas accommodatis
Pars prima
Hoc opus, Hoc Carmen quod cernis
Thamite Lector Alcuinus Domini
Fecit Honore sui.[49]

Illustration 13

Uses of the psalms

Alcuin was a great teacher, and master of many teachers who subsequently taught in various universities across Europe. He was born in 735, in York, seventy five miles south of Jarrow. In 766 he was appointed master of the Cathedral in York. Fifteen years later (781) he met the Emperor Charlemagne (742-814), who invited him to Aachen, Germany, as administrator of religious reform as he was anxious to have the empire Christianised, hence the Holy Roman Empire, Alcuin accepted. Charlemagne promoted the retention of Latin and was helped by Alcuin to produce a one volume bible. Northumbria at this time had two very important monasteries, Wearmouth and Jarrow, with Coelfrith (died 716) abbot of both. Benedict Biscop (d. 690), an Englishman when visiting Rome had acquired a bible of St. Jerome's translation which had been transcribed by Cassiodorus and brought it back to England. Coelfrith said that three vast manuscripts were made on the same model, one each for Coelfrith's two monasteries, Wearmouth and Jarrow and one for the Pope in Rome. Coelfrith intended to deliver it, but died on his way to Rome, the manuscript however survived.

In 796 Alcuin became abbot of St. Martin's Abbey in Tours and a Bible was sent to him from York, 797. It was then transcribed in the *scriptoria* of the monastery of Tours and many copies were produced over the following years, even after his death. It is claimed that the output was "two bibles every year for 50 years", with copies by the mid-ninth century at Laon, Aachen, Paris, St. Denis, Metz, St. Gall.

Every Cistercian abbey had a copy of the norms of the chant, and the source, or the library, from which this *Expositio Sti Augustini Psalmis* was obtained is not known.

The scribe has written forty six lines, and in doing so has abbreviated them. However the full text has been published by Migne.[50] He may have done so, to fit the "uses" into the parchment, or being aware that the daily office was already arranged by the Order, chose to write a synopsis according to the needs of the monks, or he may have copied it word for word from the manuscript which he had been given for that purpose.

Use 1   *Si vis pro peccatis*, lines 1-8
Use 2   *Si vis orare*, lines 8-11
Use 3   *Si vis omnipotentem* is missing
Use 4   *Si diverses tentationibus* lines 12-15
Use 5   *Si tibi vita praesens*, lines 16-18
Use 6   *Si te in tribulationibus*, lines 18-21
Use 7   *Post acceptam quietem*, lines 22-28
Use 8   *Si volueris intima*, lines 28-38
Use 9   *In psalterio usque ad obitum*, lines 38-46

In Use 1, *Si vis pro peccatis tuis poenitenticam age*, "if you wish to do penance", the monk is told that he should not use a multitude of words, but ponder and think deeply and sing the psalms of David. He recommends Psalm 6 or 37, *Domine ne in furore tuo arguas me*, Lord in thy wrath rebuke me not; *Domini exaudi*, Lord hear my prayer, Psalm 101; *Beati quorum remissae sunt*, Happy are those whose trespasses are forgiven, Psalm 31; *Misere mei Deus*, Be gracious to me O God, Psalm 50; *Deus, secundum magnam profundis de profundis*, Out of the depths I cry to thee O Lord, Psalm 129; and very quickly you will have the clemency of God.

The second use on the manuscript commences with *si vis orare mitte mentém tuam ad virtutem psalmorium*", if you wish to pray, allow your mind to sink into the power of the psalms. *Exaudi Domini justitiam meam*, Hear O Lord my just plea, Psalm 16; *Ad te, Domini levavi*, To Thee O Lord I raise up my soul, Psalm 24; *Deus in nominee tuo*, O God by Thy name, rescue me, Psalm 53; *Deus in adjutorium meum*, O Lord set Thy mind to help me, Psalm 69; *Inte, Domine speravi*, In Thee O Lord I put my trust, Psalm 30; *Inclina Domine aurem tuam et exaudi me*, Bend down Thine ear to me O Lord and hear me, Psalm 85.

The scribe has not included Use 3. The fourth use, if you are afflicted by all kinds of tribulations, and you are hemmed in on all sides by temptation, normal for man (human) or spiritual and you seem to be abandoned by God, who for the most part does 'abandon' his holy ones for a time to prove them and then a temptation appears to you greater than you are able to endure, then in your innermost mind say these psalms, the first of which is *Deus Deus meus, respice in me*, O God my God, look Thou upon me, Psalm 21; *Exaudi Deus, orationem meam cum deprecor*, Hear O God my prayer when I make petition, Psalm 63; *Salvum me fac Deus*, Save me O God, Psalm 68; *Et Clemens dues statem te adjuvabit, et tentationem, quam pateris, tolerare te posse efficiet* - he will make you able to tolerate the temptation which you suffer.

In manuscript 36929 only Psalms 21, 63, 68, the three psalms of David are mentioned. The fifth use advises "that if the present life is wearisome and your soul delights with ardent desire in the heavenly fatherland and the Omnipotent God, then with 'intense' mind, sing these psalms, *Quemadmodum desiderat cervus ad fontes aquarum*, As the stag longeth for the running streams, Psalm 41; *Deus Deus meus ad te de luce vigilo*, O God, My God after Thee do I long in the morning, Psalm 62.

The sixth use, "if you understand yourself to be abandoned by God in your tribulation, with contrite heart sing these psalms": *Usquequo Domine*, How long O Lord, Psalm 12; *In te domine speravi*, To Thee O Lord, I put my trust, Psalm 30; *Deus auribus nostris audivimus*, O God we have heard with our own ears, Psalm 43; *Miserere mei Deus*, be gracious to me O God, Psalm 50; *Exaudi Deus deprecationem meam*, Hear O God my crying, Psalm 60. Here the scribe has recorded a different order, namely Psalm 12, 43, 50, 60, 30 to the above quoted (12, 30, 43, 50, 60). The seventh use "at all times, every day, every hour, whether of prosperity or tribulation, always sing the hymn of the three boys (in the furnace) [hence no one is able to explain the power of the name in which every creature is invited to praise the Creator]", *Benedicam Dominum in omni tempore*, The Lord I will praise at all times, Psalm 33.

The eighth use of the psalms, "If you wish to exercise yourself in your inmost mind in the divine praises and precepts and in heavenly commandment, then sing Blessed (or how happy) those of blameless lives and though you contemplate and scrutinize the power of this psalm right up to the end of your life, you will never I think, be able to understand it perfectly. In which, there is no verse, but that in it, either way of God or a law, or commandment, or precept of God, or words, or justifications, or discourses and therefore there is no need for you to diffuse your soul through different books", *Beati immaculati in via: qui ambulant in lege Domini*, Happy are the stainless in life's way, Psalm 118.

The ninth use, "In the psalter alone up to the end of your life, you have matter for reading, for discerning (searching), teaching and praying, in which you will find precepts, evangelical and apostolic and all the divine books, spiritually and intelligently, to some extent treated (commented on) and describing the first coming (advent) of Our Lord, you will find foretold (prophesied) also the Incarnation, Passion, Resurrection, Easter *et omnem virtuem divinorum dictorum in psalmis invenies. In psalterio usque ad obitum vitae tuae habes materiam legendi, scrutandi, docendi; in quo invenies propheticos, evangelicos, atque apostolicos, atque omnes divinos libros spiritualiter, ad quem intelligitur [Forte, atque intelligibiliter] ex parte tractatos atque descriptos, et priorem atque secundum adventum Domini ibi reperies prophetatos. In carnationem quoque et passionem, resurrectionemque, atque ascensionem Dominicam, et omnem, virtutem divinorum dictorum in psalmis invenies.*

It is helpful to use the Migne edition, to understand the parchment transcription in MS 36929, as I have done in this account.

Cassiodorus

Cassiodorus (c.480-580) was an editor and promoter of the Bible. He was a Roman Senator, who in his mid fifties, retired from the Civil Service and founded a monastery on his family estate near Naples. On it was a fish pond and the monastery was named after it, the Vivarium (fish pond). In his role as editor, he did not alter the text, but selected the translations with care and standardized the grammar and spelling and he wrote a textbook called the *Institutions*, on Christian education.

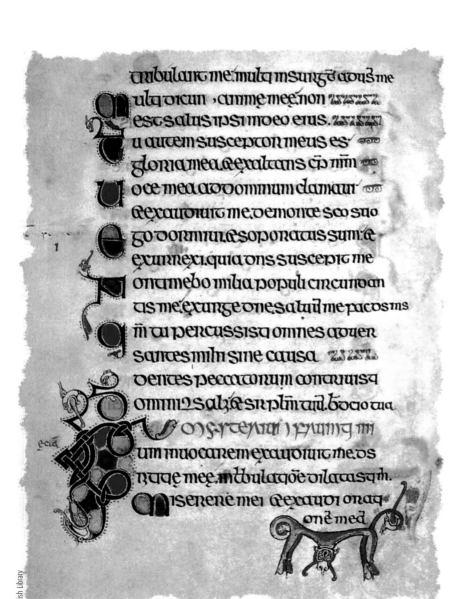

Illustration 14 - Psalm 3 & 4
Psalm 4, for the choir leader: On stringed instruments, as psalm of David. When I call on Him just God heareth me. When I was straitened Thou didst set me at large, Be gracious to me and hear my prayer.

The "divisions of Cassiodorus" are mentioned in the margins of the first seven psalms. In his commentary (*Expositio*), Cassiodorus has a uniform approach for his treatment of each psalm: first the biblical heading, if there is one, or words on why there is no heading, then some general words without any heading. After this comes a section under the heading *Diuisio psalm* on the content of the psalms, who is speaking in it, next comes a section headed *Expositio psalm*, with a word for word, or phrase by phrase explanation of the entire psalm and the work generally ends with a section headed *Conclusio psalm*. The divisions as noted in the first seven psalms may refer to relevant sections of Cassiodorus' work (see photo – Psalm 1).

The psalms were never numbered, never modernized, the psalter was always a single volume work. They were recited from the opening word,

Illustration 15 - Psalm 1
*Fortunate is the man
who hath not walked according to the
counsel with the godless;
Nor stood in the path of sinners
Nor sat in the chair of corruption.*

and had open capitals, painted red or blue, visual mnemonics, monks could recognise these coloured headings and know where they were at. The large initial needed to be seen at a distance of two feet in a dark candlelit church in winter before sunrise or late evening. There are twenty two lines to each folio and some lines are continued with doodles, oscillating semi-circles. The same occurs in St. Jerome's Hebrew Bible, in which case it may be said that the Irish monk was repeating a tradition (see photo – psalm).

However, there are some zoomorphs in this manuscript 36929, but even the Great Bible of Citeaux evades the famous Article 82 of the Statutes of Citeaux and occasionally introduces grotesque animal heads, as if the *Apologia* had never been written. This Great Bible of Citeaux was executed upon St. Bernard's orders and represents the purest type of Cistercian manuscript.

In this manuscript 36929 the scribe has framed the words "With ten stringed psaltery and harp, with zither accompanied song" (Psalm 91) with a double series of zigzag strokes (see photo). Psalm 96 has the letter 'I' portrayed as a vertical shaped

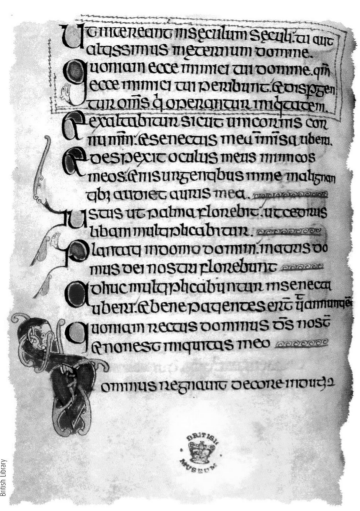

Saint Bernard instructing Aelred to write
the Treatise 'Mirror of Charity'

fish and Psalm 100 has a face, with nimbus around the head, which I take as a portrait of Christ, "a mirror, for rulers". There was a lot of interest on "mirror" for example "Mirror of Faith" William Theiry, "Mirror of Charity" Aelred, "A Mirror for monks" Blosius. A folio separated Psalm 50 from Psalm 51, the page is framed with interlacing, however in the top left hand corner, is the *Dextera Dei*, the hand of God in blessing with the index finger and the middle one outstretched, and the little finger crossing over and the fourth finger crossing under. The scribe has inserted titles as in Psalm 51, but another scribe has inserted a title on Psalm 99, and the contrast is remarkable, the letters are of different sizes and crushed into the space – *Quia mirabilia fecit Dominus* and there are many other examples such as occurs between Psalms 79 and 80.

Illustration 16
Psalm 91,
With ten stringed psaltry and harp with zither
accompanied song verse 4

Tis that they may but vanish forever; verse 8

But Thou, Most high, art forever; verse 9.

Yea, verily, Thy enemies, O Lord
Yea verily, Thy enemies perish
All evil-doers are scattered; verse 10

Illustration 17 *The Piper:*
Red hair, dressed in saffron, green and black;
Genuflecting, and playing the bagpipes.
From the Ordinal of Rosglas

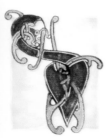

Illustration 18 - *Psalm 100*
A psalm of David
Of graciousness and right I would sing,
To Thee O Lord I would chant I would give thought to the Perfect way
When wilt Thou come to me?

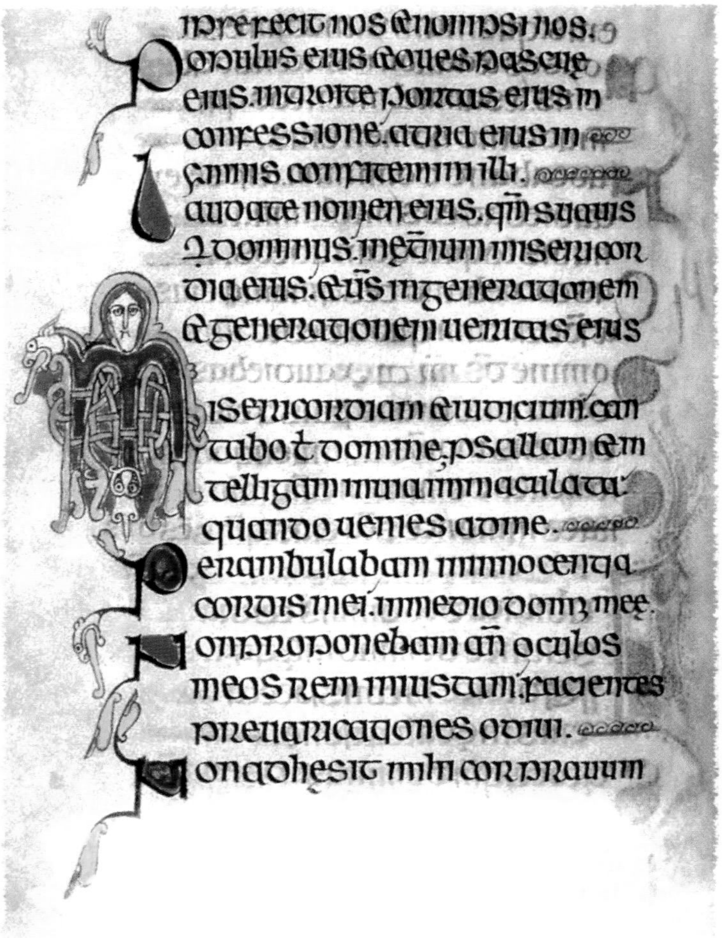

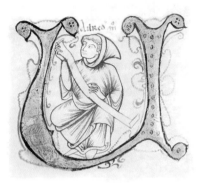

British Library

St Aelred

British Library

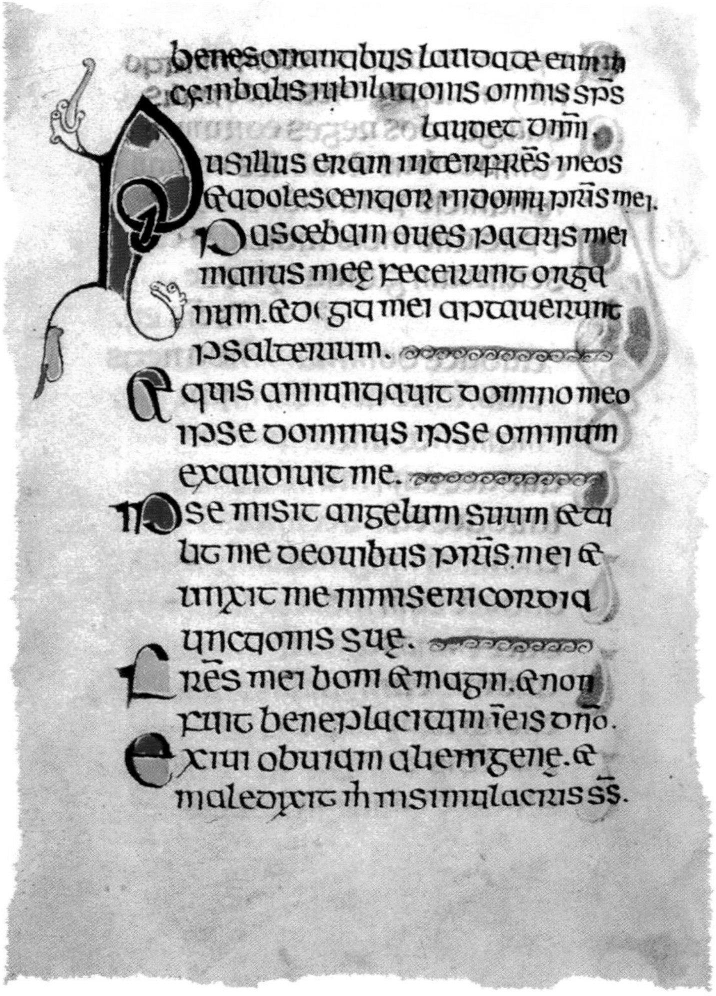

Illustration 19 - *Psalm 150 and Psalm 151*
There is a text:

Pusillus eram inter fratres meos
(I was a little one amongst my brothers)
Et adolescentior, in domu, patris mei
(and a younger 'adolescent' in the house of my father)
Pascebam oues patris mei
(I used herd the sheep of my father)
Manus meae facerunt organum et digite mei aptaverunt psalterium
(My hands made an 'organ' and my fingers fashioned a psaltery)
Et quis annuntiavit Domino Meo
(and who announced to my Lord)
Ipse Dominus ipse omnium exaudivit me
(The Lord Himself He of all heard me)
Ipse misit angelum suum et tulit me deovibus prioris mei et unxit me in misericordia unctionis suae
(He himself sent his angel).

In the passage, the words *psalterium* and *organum* occur. In the Hebrew text David said that he made two musical instruments, "ugab" (musical instrument) and kinnon (a lyre). The Greek translates "ugab" as *organon* (musical instrument) and *psalterson*. The Latin takes over both words as *organum* and *psalterium*. The Hebrew "ugab" is translated as flute. Over the centuries, by extension the meaning was changed and by the thirteenth century came to be identified as a musical form.

Psalmody comes from the Greek quote *Psalmodia* which means singing to the harp whilst *Psalmos* from Greek means music of a stringed instrument and psaltery, an ancient and medieval stringed instrument like the zither, played by plucking. A High Cross called the Ballyogan Cross now in the precincts of Duiske Abbey, County Kilkenny, depicts David with his harp – the Irish word for the harp is cruit and was of a small rather than a floor model type. There is a record of an organ in the sale of chattels of the same abbey in the "Extents of Irish Monastic Possessions 1541" and in the Ordinal of Rosglas (Monasterevin) on a folio, there is a drawing of a piper. Oral tradition in this area as recorded by O'Leary says that "Aengus a monk of Holy Cross Abbey, instructed Lord Milo Roche, bishop of Leighlin (who could play many instruments) to play the harp and that he repaired the 'Old wind organ' which had not been used for years, and had been affected by damp and the bellows gnawed by rats". It is true that Duiske Abbey possessed an organ, but the source for this quotation cannot be found. There was a family, called Harpur, who were bards who came from Gloucestershire to Ireland as Anglo-Norman adventurers who built Harperstown Castle, near Taghmon, County Wexford. In 1278, mention is made of David, son of Stephen the Harper, as there is a quit claim record whereby he gave land called Coppenagh to the monks of Duiske Abbey for six silver marks.

The monk Aengus (again citing O'Leary and Oral tradition) "excels in music, not alone is he versed in psalms and choir basses, witness his setting of *Benedicam Dominum*, but he too plays the cruit – the Abbot of Duiske was not in favour of his playing because the brethren are apt to forget complain". Can oral tradition be ignored in a Church which has an unbroken service of Mass celebration since 1204?

The Harp or Cruit

Many melodies today owe their preservation to the Cistercians alone, which have the long *sup spun milisma* (Greek word meaning chant) in which the melody as it were overflows the text; and *Jubilus*, a series of notes that constitutes a melodic development, freed from words which St. Augustine explains as an 'overflow of the heart which is too enraptured to find words for expression'.

"Gaudium verbis non explicare et tamen voce testari quod intus conceptum est et explicare non potest: hoc est jubilare."

Gregorian chant is pre-eminently a verbal music, it has no existence apart from words, it forms an intimate and integral part of it. It is never set to music, the music must spring out of the word in which it lies latent. Expression in plain chant is not emotional nor theatrical, it is how to pray, to meditate, to mourn, to jubilate (see 9 uses of psalms).

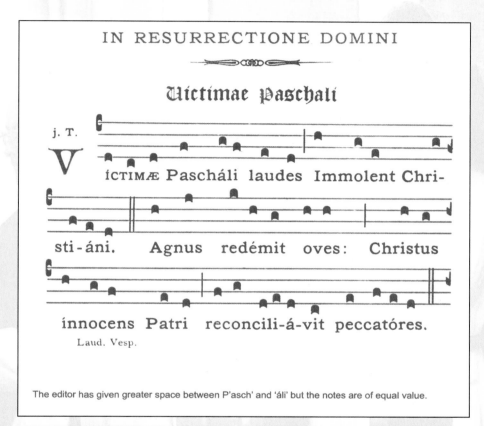

IN RESURRECTIONE DOMINI

Victimae Paschali

j. T. Víctimæ Pascháli laudes Immolent Chri-

sti-áni. Agnus redémit oves: Christus

ínnocens Patri reconcili-á-vit peccatóres.

Laud. Vesp.

The editor has given greater space between P'asch' and 'áli' but the notes are of equal value.

Illustration 20
This melody is still sung by the Cistercians today. The editor has given greater space between P, asch and 'áli' but the notes are of equal value.

After Sturman, P.
Advanced harmony, melody and composition.

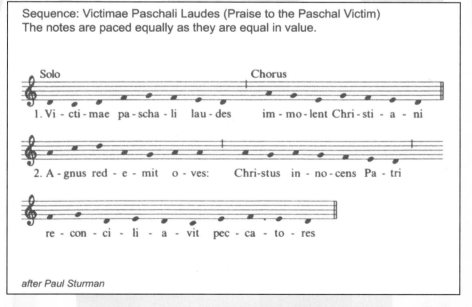

Sequence: Victimae Paschali Laudes (Praise to the Paschal Victim)
The notes are paced equally as they are equal in value.

Solo   Chorus

1. Vi - cti - mae pa - scha - li lau - des   im - mo - lent Chri - sti - a - ni

2. A - gnus red - e - mit o - ves: Chri - stus in - no - cens Pa - tri

re - con - ci - li - a - vit pec - ca - to - res

after Paul Sturman

The Colophon of Cormac

This passage *'Pusillus eram'* refers to David, who was chosen by Samuel (the Prophet) in preference to his older and more presentable six brothers in the eyes of man, but not of God. All of this has allusions to the Prophet Samuel and his anointing of David (16:1, 6-7, 10-13) where the youngest son of Jesse, David is called in from the herding of sheep and chosen to be anointed before his six bigger and older brothers, ending with David's contest with Goliath, in this psalter, it is continued onto Psalm 150, there is no break between them. It is probably an amalgam of two distinct Hebrew psalms, of which the first (dealing with the anointing of David) and part of the second (on the combat with Goliath) have been found in Qumram Cave II, in 1966. The Hebrew text was translated into Greek and in the *Septuagint* it is headed: This psalm is a genuine psalm of David, though supernumerary, composed when he fought with Goliath. From the Greek the psalm was translated into Latin as in this Gallican Psalter 36929.

Today this is not included in the canon of psalms, although the Cistercians used the second half as a responsary for the lessons for 1st Nocturne of the 4th Sunday after Pentecost and may be found in the old Latin Cistercian Breviary:

> *Deus omnium exauditor est: Ipse misit Angelum suum, et tulet me de ovibus patris mei: et unxit me untione misericordiae suae.*

I am aware of the existence of a seventh century text Cormac's Psalter but this Cistercian scribe Cormac may have been comparing his own family life, his vocation, his love of music with that of David's.

David Howlett, Peritia 8 (1995) 81-91

The Polyphonic Colophon to Cormac's Psalter has considered this as poetry and in the interest of accuracy and in acknowledging his scholarship, I have decided to quote his work as it gives a thorough understanding and appreciation of the words of Cormac and their suitability for setting to music.

> Cormacus scripsit hoc ψsalterium ora pro eo.
> Qui legis hec ora pro sese qualibet hora.

> Cormac wrote this Psalter; pray for him.

You who read these things, pray for himself [perhaps meaning 'yourself'] in every hour.

Here are two lines of dactylic hexameter verse, which both exhibit correct quantities, with two elisions in the first line in *psalterium ora* and *pro eo*, with nothing extraordinary in the second. Both verses exhibit internal vowel rhymes in the third and the sixth feet. In the first compare the *o* in *hoc* with that in *eo*. In the second compare the *i*, , *e*, and *ora* in *legis hec ora* with those in *qualibet hora*.

The second verse also exhibits internal alliteration on *qu* and *l* in *qui legis* and *qualibet*. Both verses exhibit chiastic disposition of sounds. In the first, around the central *o* in *hoc* in the third foot, compare the *ps-t* of *scripsit* with that of *psalterium*, the *ri* of *scripsit* with that of *psalterium*, the *u* of *Cormacus* with that of *psalterium*, and the *or-a* of *Cormacus* with that of *ora*. The first and last of these chiastically disposed sounds in the first verse are echoed at the centre of the second verse. Around the central *a* of *ora* in the third foot, compare the *r* of *ora* with that of *pro*, the *o* of *ora* with that of *pro*, the *e* of *hec* with that of *sese*, the *s* of *legis* with that of *sese*, the *i* of *legis* with that of *qualibet*, and the *e* of *legis* with that of *qualibet*. The first verse is linked to the second by parallelism of *Cormacus scripsit hoc* with *qui legis hec* and of *ora pro eo* with *ora pro sese*.[5]

Cōrmācūs scrīpsīt hōc ψsāltĕrĭum ōrā prō ęō .
Quī lĕgĭs hēc ōrā prō sēsē quālĭbĕt hōrā .

Cormacus scripsit hoc ψsalterium ora pro eo
*Qu*i *l*egis hec *ora* pro sese **qual***i*bet hora

cORmACUs scRIPSiT hOc PSalTeRIUm ORA pro eo
qui lEgIs hEc ORA pRO sEse qualIbEt hora

Following conventions of composition observed by scores of Celtic Latin authors from the fifth century to the sixteenth,[6] Cormac refers to himself and his work in places determined by calculation of sesquioctave ratio 1⅛:1 (reckoned one way 9:8 and reckoned another way 1/9 and 8/9). Let us note the references to Cormac himself. The fifteen words of the colophon divide by sesquioctave ratio at 8 and 7, at the end of the first verse, *eo*. The twenty-nine syllables divide by sesquioctave ratio at 15 and 14, at *eo*. The seventy letters divide by sesquioctave ratio at 37 and 33, at *eo*. The fifteen words divide by one-ninth at 1.67, the twenty-nine syllables at 3, and the seventy letters at 8. the first word names the writer *Cormacus* in three syllables and eight letters. Let us note also the references to Cormac's work. From *hoc psalterium* to *qui legis hec* inclusive there are eight words, fourteen syllables, and thirty-two letters.

The reader is invited to pray for Cormac at *ora*, the fifth word from the beginning of the colophon, and for himself at *ora*, the fifth word from the end. Between *ora* and *ora* there are five words. Before the former *ora* there are ten syllables. From the latter *ora* inclusive to the end there are ten syllables. From the first syllable of the former *ora* to the first syllable of the latter *ora* inclusive there are ten syllables.

5 I print the lines three times to exhibit various features. In the first, capital letters and punctuation marks in boldface represent features of the manuscript. I have added scansion marks. In the second, italics represent internal rhyme and bold italics represent internal alliteration. In the third, upper case represents chiastic disposition of sounds; bold italics represent parallelism of idea between verses.

6 D.R. Howlett, 'Some criteria for editing Abaelard', *Archivium Latinitatis Medii Aevi* 51 (1993) 197-202; id. 'Boethian music in Donnchadh's *carmen*', *Ériu* 44 (1993) 187-88; id. *Liber epistolarum sancti Patricii episcopi: the book of letters of Saint Patrick the bishop* (Dublin 1994); id. *The Celtic Latin tradition of biblical style* (Dublin 1995); id. *British books in biblical style* (Dublin 1996); id. 'Five experiments in textual reconstruction and analysis', above 1-50.

I am grateful to Rev. Prof. Martin McNamara for drawing my attention to this essay after I spoke about MS36929 in Kalamazoo (May 2005).
Music from Abbey Assaroe, Co. Donegal (fd. 1178 + 1597)
- another musical link with the past.

Illustration 21
The music of Abbey Assaroe, Co. Donegal
Permission © Bethelem Abbey
This music is presently used in Mt. St. Joseph Abbey, Roscrea for the chanting of Psalm 50 at Lauds on Sundays and for Psalm 4 at Compline on Monday, Wednesday, Friday in Our Lady of Bolton Abbey, Moone, Co. Kildare.

Illustration 21
*The music of Abbey
Assaroe, Co. Donegal*
Permission © Bethelem Abbey

Photo 27 -
*Carved stones from
the ruins of Abbey
Assaroe built into
the graveyard wall*

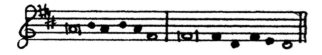

'....... *where the very stones
once sang the psalms*'.

G Carville

Having read 'Manuscript Illumination' by Dr. Michelle Browne (British Library) I decided to consult her about Royal 2.A.XX.f.17 as to how similar this folio from a Prayer book was to MS36929 and she replied as follows:
"The script is a later Irish Insular miniscule with a formal rounded aspect perhaps influenced by European Romanesque textualis hands (see also the Book of Armagh)".

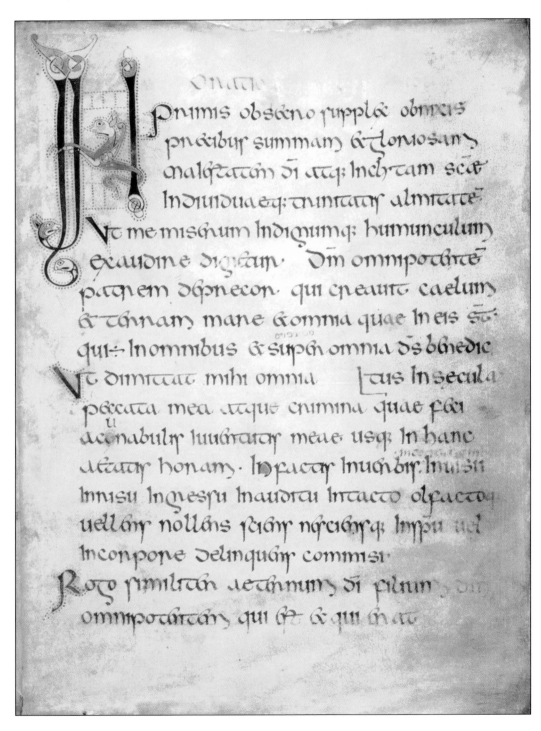

Illustration 22 Royal 2.A.XX.f.17

Illustration 23a

*Brackets denote tape recorder count

Unseen – sight reading original folio (not transposed)

Bro. Finbar (Cantor)
Our Lady of Bethlehem Abbey
Portglenone, County Antrim
30 March 2005

Cormacus scripsit hoc psalterium ora pro eo
Verse 1 lines one and two, doh clef same as verse 2
Line 3 change of doh clef

Qui legis haec ora pro sese qualibet hora
Verse 2 lines one and two, same as verse 1
Line 3 same change of doh clef as in verse 1

"Testing" – "will recorder be recording at right speed?"

"I will check" [stop]
"Everything seems to be in order"

"We shall proceed"

"I will just sing the last line first, it seems to be easier, it is more clearly printed"

"Qui legis haec ora pro sese qualibet hora" [844/848]

"I'm taking it as the 8th tone"

"Qui legis haec ora pro sese qualibet hora" [849/852]

"I'll do it quicker – again"

"It sounds more like the 8th mode when I'm doing it that way"

"Qui legis haec ora pro sese qualibet hora" [853/856]

"And the other bit above is *cormacus scripsit hoc psalterium ora pro eo*" [857/863]

"Ora pro eo is a bit confusing" [863/864]
"Cormacus scripsit hoc – that's wrong" [865/866]

"Cormacus scripsit hoc psalterium ora pro eo" [870/874]

"Hoc psalterium ora pro eo" [874/876]

"It is hard to know which words should be accepted, some of the little notes have tails, slight tails on them. I will try that again."

"Qui legis haec ora pro sese qualibet hora, sese qualibet hora" [880/884]

"Cormacus scripsit hoc psalterium ora pro eo" [886/888]

"See, there are smudges on this" (folio)

"Now, I'll try and sing the other music, that has the blank things written underneath it"

"It is much more elaborate actually"

"La la la la la la la la la la la la la la la la la la la la la la la la la la" [892/897]

"That was the top one and I'll do this one. Below Cormac, which seems to be the start of the second stanza of the hymn or whatever you would call the thing, it is the 7th tone, by the way, this sounds like the 7th tone, the other bit sounds like the 8th tone. What we call the tones or modes whatever"
"La la la la la" [902/907]

"That one is not as clear as the other. So really there is another line here, too, I'll try below Cormac, the line below Cormac, it seems to be clearer, the stanza below the second part."
"La la la la la la la la la la la la la la la la la" [912/915]

"Now that bit there could be a bar, a tiny break, a tiny breather."
"La la la la la la la la la la la la la la la la la la la la la la la la la la la" [916/923]

"And if my transposition of the key signatures or whatever you call that business at the front, it would start off on the same note again."
"La la la la la la la la la" [925/927]

"Qui legis haec ora pro sese qualibet hora" [928/930]

"I'll do that whole section again."
"La la la la la la la la la la la la la la la la la la la la la la la la la la la la la la la la la la la la la la la la la la" [931/939]

"Qui legis haec ora pro sese qualibet hora" [939/941]

"I really can't do much better than that. It is a matter of conjecture. I will leave it at that – I might try to get the post in time."

"Cormacus scripsit hoc psalterium ora pro eo
Qui legis haec ora pro sese qualibet hora"

Illustration A is from Manuscript 36929

Illustration B is the same music in Gregorian chant

Illustration C is the same music transposed into modern staff notation

Illustration D is the same music transposed into modern staff notation with a common time signature

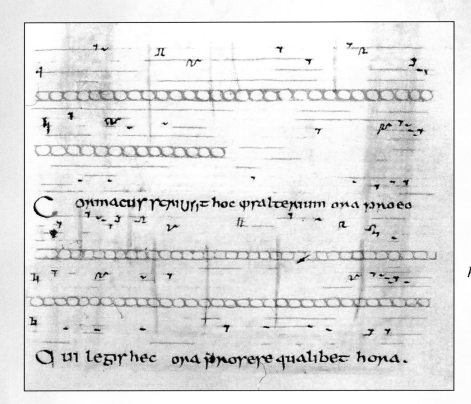

Illustration 23A – *Manuscript 36929 has 'moving' doh clef in both verses. There are no bar lines but the scribe has drawn red lines to fit the syllables to the notes.*

Illustration 23b – *The same music in Gregorian Chant*

notice change of doh clef E F and G, bar 6 F, bar 13 J have a H J and Z. Bar 1 has a descending group of small diamond shaped notes called conjunctura, longa and breve which do not have a fixed duration. "Bar 5" is different from "Bar 12", a note has been left out in "bar 5" which may be a breathing aid.

There are melismas in "bar 1 E", "bar 6 F".

"Bar 13 J" – many notes to one word as in "bars 1 E-F" "Cormacus", "bars 8 H" "legis".

"Bar 3 E F G" has one note of the melody to one syllable of the text – "hoc" "bar 4", "psalterium" "bar 7", "Qui" lines H J Z.

Verse 1 *Cormacus scripsit hoc psalterium ora pro eo* has 15 syllables; verse 2 *Qui legis haec ora pro sese qualibet hora* has 15 syllables. A verse is a single line, not as in poetry.

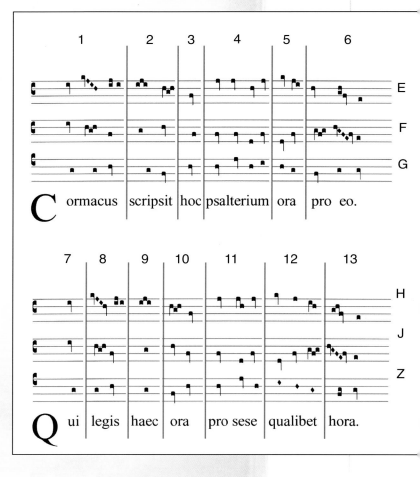

The composer has combined two melodically independent lines using oblique and contrary motion.
The Plain Chant is in the lower voice but each note is prolonged to allow the upper voices to sing
against it. The lower voice has lost its original character as a definite tune making it a series of single
drone-like notes (see illustration 8, page 54).

Illustration 23C – *Music transposed*
into modern staff notation
Music note the insertion of division 1-6,
7-13 and reference to line nominations E
F G and H J Z for reference. Lines G Z
have plain chant in the lower voice, each
note is prolonged so as to allow the
upper voices to sing phrases of varying
length, for example:
"1 E" and "1 F"
"6 E" and "6 F"
"8 H" and "8 J"
"9 H" and "9 J"
"10 H" and "10 J"
"11 H" and "11 J"

Contrary notation is shown in:
"2 F" and "2 G"
"5 F" and "5 G"
"10 J" and "10 Z"
"11 J" and "11 Z"
"12 J" and "12 Z"

Unison is reached in bars 6 E F G and in
bars 13 H J Z. The ending 13 Z dips on
the second last syllable.

Illustration D – modern notation, with key signature and time signature, shows the grouping of notes and intervals in treble for soprano.

There are intervals of 5th; 4th; 6th; 7th with 4th, 5th, octaves, the most prominent. Cormac has combined three melodically independent lines, using oblique and contrary motion. The plain chant is in the lower voice, but each note is prolonged so as to allow the upper voices to sing against it. The lower voice has not retained its original character as a definite tune, making it a series of single drone like notes. This is *florid organum* which is surprising as many people claim that the Cistercians only sang plain chant and not polyphony.

Conclusion

By now, with the evidence obtained from two medieval manuscript sources transcribed in Ireland, by Irish monks, letters from St. Bernard to Dermot McMurrough, King of Leinster and to St. Malachy, maps, illustrations, photographs, tables, diagrams, one begins to glimpse the enormously influential role of the Cistercian Order in their thirty three abbey churches in Medieval Ireland.

The first Irish Cistercian monks were trained in Saint Bernard's Abbey, Clairvaux and the necessary manuscripts for the Office in Mellifont Abbey were brought from that monastery too.

They erected the greatest buildings in the Ireland of their time, in architecture new to this country. Their monastic churches were built to a standard plan made of squares for the 'Order of Citeaux', which was sent by Saint Bernard from his Abbey of Clairvaux for the building of Mellifont Abbey. The erection and supervision was undertaken by the French Monk Robert.

I have explained how the ratio of the chords is reflected in the layout of the Abbey Churches so that there is perfect symmetry or harmony in the architectural plan echoing the chant and their attention given to acoustics. Their methods of sight singing (from the Ordinal of Rosglas) and their musical instruments have been described.

In conclusion, the three secrets of the Cistercians were that of light, that of number and that of sound. Their use of the Gothic method of vaulting gave a light filled sanctuary, the oratorium became an ecclesia, a place less for the praying monks than for the presence of the worshipped God, the ratio of the chords in music gave perfect symmetry and harmony to the Cistercian architectural plan and they adopted acoustic methods to accentuate the clarity of the antiphonal singing of the choirs.

The coming of the Cistercians to Ireland in 1142 has been recorded by some as sounding the death knell of the Celtic monasticism that is one of the glories of European history, but in reality, it reopened Ireland's contacts with Europe on a broader basis, at religious, cultural, economic and musical levels.

Monasterevin (Rosea Vallis, Rosglas)

In the charter of the twelfth century (Dugdale, ii, 1031-2) Dermot O'Dempsey, King of Offaly, granted and confirmed the site and possessions (enumerated) to the monks of Rosglas in honour of Blessed Mary and St. Benedict; no order is mentioned and the first two witnesses are Nehemias, bishop of Kildare (from 1177) and Donat (Dungal), bishop of Leighlin, who died in 1181: HBC. This charter must therefore be dated between 1177 and 1181. Ware and ALS give 1178 as the date of colonisation from Baltinglass. The inclusion of the name of St. Benedict in the charter and these two distinct dates 1177 and 1181 may mean that the monastery was founded in 1178 for Irish monks O.S.B. who wished to be and lived as Cistercians, their official affiliation being delayed until 1189. The founder died in 1193 (AU) and John abbot of Monasterevin became bishop of Leighlin 1197 (HBC). The Annals of St. Mary's Abbey, Dublin (Cistercian) gives the date as 22 October 1189 as the colonisation from Baltinglass. This is the date of their official affiliation.

Date recorded on the Ordinal of Rosglas 1509.

Gwynn & Hadcock Medieval Religious Houses 1970.

Appendix 2

"Sing 150 Psalms" St. Benedict MS36929 – Contents

Psalm	Office	Page numbers (as on print from microfilm)	Remarks
1	Monday Prime		
2	Monday Prime	4-5	
3	Sun/Mon/Tues/Wed/Thu/Fri/Sat Vigils	5-6	
4	Monday Compline		
	Song of David	6-7	Divisions of Cassiodorus
	"Know ye what the Lord has done for us"		
5	Monday Lauds	8-9	"Prophets"
6	1st Penitential, Monday Prime	9-11	"Antiphon: Vide Domine Afflicitone"
	Divisions of Cassiodorus		
7	Tuesday Prime	11-12-13	Words of antiphon prefixed
8	Tuesday Prime	13-14	
9(a)	Tuesday Prime	14-15-16	Variation in Latin (present-tense, instead of past tense)
9(b)	Wednesday Prime	16-17-18-19	
10	Wednesday Prime	19-20	Title
11	Wednesday Prime	20-21	
12	Thursday Prime	21-22	Title, allegorical
13	Thursday Prime	22-23	
14	Thursday Prime	23-24	
15	Friday Prime	26	Words of antiphon prefixed
16	Friday Prime	26-27-28	Title
17(a)	Friday Prime	28-29-30-31	"The Lord is my strength" a theme of a psalm, middle verse, out of the apocalypse, words of the antiphon prefixed
17(b)	Saturday Prime	34-35-36-37	
18	Saturday Prime	37-38-39	"The Heavens proclaim"
	words of antiphon prefixed		
19	Saturday Prime ends	40	Prime; line repeated; commentary heading words of antiphon prefixed – what the monks should think about
20	Sunday Vigils	40-41-42	
21	Sunday Vigils	42-43-44-45	Words of antiphon prefixed
22	Sunday Vigils	46-47	
23	Sunday Vigils	47-48-49	
24	Sunday Vigils	49-50-51	
25	Sunday Vigils	51-52	
26	Sunday Vigils	53-54-55	Words of antiphon prefixed
27	Sunday Vigils	55-56-57	

Psalm	Office	Page numbers (as on print from microfilm)	Remarks
28	Sunday Vigils	57-58	
29	Sunday Vigils	58-59-60	
30	Sunday Vigils	60-61-62-63	
31	Sunday Vigils	64-65	
32	Monday Vigils	65-66-67-68	
33	Monday Vigils	68-69-70-71	
34	Monday Vigils	71-72-73-74-75	
35	Monday Lauds	75-76	
36(a)	Monday Vigils	76-77-78-79-80	
36(b)	Monday Vigils	80-81	
37	Monday Vigils	81-82-83-84	
38	Monday Vigils	85-86	
39	Monday Vigils	87-88-89-90	
40	Monday Vigils	90-91-92	
41	Monday Vigils	92-93-94	
42	Tuesday Lauds		
43	Monday Vigils	95-96-97-98-99	
44	Monday Vigils	100-101	
45	Tuesday Vigils	101-102-103	
46	Tuesday Vigils	103-104	
47	Tuesday Vigils	104-105	
48	Tuesday Vigils	105-106-107-108	
49	Tuesday Vigils	109-110-111	
50	Sun/Mon/Tues/Wed/Thu/Fri/Sat Lauds 111-112-113		Voice of penance
Canticle	Daniel 3	114-115-116	
Canticle	Isiaih	116	
Canticle	Ezechial	117-118	

End of Division 1

Psalm	Office	Page numbers	Remarks
51	Tuesday Vigils	121-122-123	Title "Quid"
52	Tuesday Vigils	123-124	
53	Tuesday Vigils	124-125	
54	Tuesday Vigils	125-126-127-128	
55	Tuesday Vigils	129-130-131	
56	Tuesday Lauds	131-132-133	
57	Tuesday Vigils	133-134	No more titles
58	Tuesday Vigils	134-135-136-137	
59	Wednesday Vigils	137-138-139	
60	Wednesday Vigils	139-140	New handwriting insertion
61	Wednesday Vigils	140-141-142	
62	Sunday Lauds	142-143-144	
63	Wednesday Lauds	144-145	
64	Wednesday Lauds	146-147	
65	Wednesday Vigils	148-149-150	
66	Sun/Mon/Tue/Wed/Thu/Fri/Sat Lauds150-151		

Psalm	Office	Page numbers (as on print from microfilm)	Remarks
67(a)	Wednesday Vigils	151-152-153	"Bless the Lord all ye people" has been inserted
67(b)	Wednesday Vigils	153-154-155-156	
68(a)	Wednesday Vigils	156-157-158-159	
68(b)	Wednesday Vigils	160-161	
69	Wednesday Vigils	161-162	
70	Wednesday Vigils	162-163-164-165	
71	Wednesday Vigils	166-167-168	
72	Wednesday Vigils	168-169-170-171	
73	Thursday Vigils	172-173-174-175	Antiphon "De Judeo"
74	Thursday Vigils	175-176	
75	Friday Lauds	176-177-178	
76	Thursday Vigils	179-180	Including antiphon, strange this is at the end of Psalm 76 "*Liberati … hereditatis*" sequence. No antiphon marked for the first two psalms for Thursday Vigils. None at end of first psalm of Nocturn. Why is it placed before Psalm 74? Antiphon, Thematic, supposed to be expressive of the psalms. Cantor introduced it at the end, the Cantor intoned the same antiphon, all joined in.
77(a)	Thursday Vigils		
77(b)	Thursday Nocturn	180-181-182-183-184-186-188-189	Divided Benedict in his rule says: Psalm will be divided here
		190	Antiphon only at end of psalms "*Inclinate aurem restanu in verba orus mei*". This is a Lenten one.
78	Thursday Vigils	190-191-192	
79	Thursday Vigils	192-193-194	Antiphon from Psalm 78, comes after Psalm 79. during the year a liturgical antiphon to cover three psalms, i.e. their liturgical arrangement. For big Feasts, every Psalm has its own antiphon; for Ordinary time, one antiphon might be for several psalms.
80	Thursday Vigils	194-195-196	
81	Thursday Vigils	196-197	
82	Thursday Vigils	197-198-199	Three psalms grouped
83	Thursday Vigils	199-200-201	No antiphon
84	Thursday Vigils	201-202-203	No antiphon
85	Friday Vigils	203-204	

86	Friday Vigils	204-205-206-207	"Bend down your ear to me and hear me, because I am here". No antiphon.
87	Thursday Lauds	207-208-209	No antiphon
88	Friday Vigils	210-211-212-213-214-215-216	No antiphon
89	Thursday Lauds	216-217-218-219	
90	Compline	219-220-221	
91	Friday Lauds	221-222-223	The scribe has drawn a zigzag this
92	Friday Vigils	222-223	"The Lord reigns and is clothed with beauty"
93	Friday Vigils	223-224-225-226	
94	Sun/Mon/Tue/Wed/Thu/Fri/Sat Vigils	226-227	"*Phoremus coram Domino Deo, nostro qui feat nos*" and "*quonram non repellet Dominum pelbem sunt Qui fecit nos and Quoruam upsus est mare et ipse fecit illtud et aridam*" – omitted capital "H"odie (hodie) is not decorated.
95	Friday Vigils	228-229	
96	Friday Vigils	229-230-231	
97	Friday Vigils	231-232	
98	Friday Vigils	233	
Canticle "*Exortatio ad Dei laudem*"			Moses/Aaron

End of Division 2

		233	The scribe returns to Moses and Aaron
99	Friday Vigils	233-234	"*Quia mirabilia fecit Dominus exhortation ad Dei laudem*" omitted
100	Friday Vigils	233-234	"Image of Christ"
Canticle		234-235-236	Canticle of Annae
Canticle		236-237-238-239	Canticle of Moses
Canticle		239-240-241-242	Habacus: three canticles after

Psalm 100.			
Dan III		57-58	
Isiaih XII,		1-6, XXXVIII	

101	Saturday Vigils	244-245-246-247	
102	Saturday Vigils	247-248-249-250	
103	Saturday Vigils	250-251-252-253-254	
104	Saturday Vigils	255-256-257-258-259	Division of Psalm 104
105	Saturday Vigils	260-261-262-263-264-265-266	Division of Psalm 105
106	Saturday Vigils	266-267-268-269-270-271	Twenty lines omitted between "*confiteantur*" and "*et sacrificent*"
107	Saturday Vigils	271-272-273	

108	Saturday Vigils	273-274-275-276-277	
109	Sunday Vespers	278	
110	Sunday Vespers	278-279	'A Fidelia' has been inserted
111	Sunday Vespers	279-280-281	
112	Sunday Vespers	281-282	
113	Monday Vespers	282-283-284-285	
114	Monday Vespers	285-286	
115	Monday Vespers	286	
116	Monday Vespers	286-287	
117	Sunday Lauds	287-288-289	
118	Sunday Prime Sext Tierce, Monday Prime Sext Tierce		
		290-291-292-293-294-295-296-297-298-299-300-301-302-303-304-305-306-307-308-309-310	
		Letter "A" with cross bar	
119	Monday Tierce	310-311	
120	Tuesday Tierce	311	Unusual script
121	Wednesday Tierce	312	
122	Thursday Tierce	312-313	
123	Friday Tierce	313-314-315	
124	Saturday Tierce		
125	Mon/Tue/Wed/Thu/Fri/Sat		
None		315-316	
126	Mon/Tue/Wed/Thu/Fri/Sat		
None		316-317	
127	Mon/Tue/Wed/Thu/Fri/Sat		
None	317		
128	Monday Vespers	318	
129	Tuesday Vespers	318-319	
130	Tuesday Vespers	319-320	
131	Tuesday Vespers	320-321-322	
132	Tuesday Vespers	322	
133	Sun/Mon/Tue/Wed/Thu/Fri/Sat Compline 322-323		
134	Wednesday Vespers	323-324-325	
135	Wednesday Vespers	325-326	
136	Wednesday Vespers	327-328	
137	Wednesday Vespers	328-329	
138	Thursday Vespers	329-330-331-332	Division of Psalm 138
139	Thursday Vespers	332-333-334	
140	Thursday Vespers	334-335	
141	Friday Vespers	335-336-337	
142	Saturday Lauds	337-338-339	
143(a)	Friday Vespers	339-340	Division
143(b)	Friday Vespers	341	
144(a)	Friday Vespers	341-342-343-344	
144(b)	Saturday Vespers		
145	Saturday Vespers	344-345	

146	Saturday Vespers	345-346	
147	Saturday Vespers	346-347	
148	Sun/Mon/Tue/Wed/Thu/Fri/Sat Lauds	347-348-349	
149	Sun/Mon/Tue/Wed/Thu/Fri/Sat Lauds	349-350-351	
150	Sun/Mon/Tue/Wed/Thu/Fri/Sat Lauds		"*Pusillus*" has been continued on Psalm
150			
Canticle		352	Moses, Deuteronomy
Saturday Lauds		353-354-355-356	Division
		357-358-359	Deuteronomy XXXII.V.10

"In the waste land he adopts him, In the howling desert of the wilderness He protects him, rears him, as the pupil of his eye"
End of ms 36929

Note: When a donor offered a site for an abbey, it had to be inspected by four senior abbots of the Cistercian Order. If it was suitable/unsuitable it was reported by them at the following General Chapter and the words of approval were taken from Deut XXXII.V.10

Index

A

Aachen, 65
acoustic jars, 29–40,
Aduard Monastery, 12
Advent, 47
Aengus the Culdee, 64
Aengus, monk, 72
aesthetics, Cistercian, 12
Ailred of Rievaulx, 70
Airghialla, kingdom of, 7
Alani Cisterciensis, 19
Alberic, prior of Molesme, 4
Alcuin, Abbot of St. Martin's, 1, 66
Aleth of Monthoud, 3
Ambrose, St., 41
Anaclectus schism, 42
Andrew, monk, 3
Anthony, St., 9-10
Antiphonarium, 6
antiphons, 46, 49
Archardus, monk, 21
architecture, Cistercian, 19-27
acoustics for chant, 29-40
Aaesthetics cistercian, 12
  geology, 28
  Gothic, 21
  proportions, 22, 24
  right bank of river, 11
  vaulted ceiling, 29
Aristotle, 37
Armagh Diocese, 7
Arnold, monk, 5
Artaud, monk, 5
Assaroe Abbey, 52, 54, 76-77
Assistant Cantors, role of, 45-49
Augustine of Hippo, St., 3, 19–22, 64
  commentaries on psalms, 64 - 68

B

Ballyogan Cross, 72
Baltinglass Abbey, 16, 18
Bangor, County Down, 7
bards, 72
Bartholomew, monk, 4
Bective Abbey, 14, 18
Belgium, 17
bell ringer, 2
Benedict, St., 2

Rule of, 2, 4, 60
Benedict Biscop, 65
Benedictine Order, 3-4,
Benedictus, 46, 49
Bernard, St., 3, 4, 59, 63-64
  architectural style, 21, 23, 27, 29
  blessing of, 63
  and Cistercians, 6-7
  Clairvaux library, 19
  forbids illumination, 61
  letter to King Dermot, 15-16
  and Malachy, 7, 14-15
  letter to, 14–16,
  and mathematics, 23
  and Mellifont, 8-9, 11-12, 17-18
  and music, 29, 42
Bethlehem Abbey, Portglenone, 55, 79
Bible
  Great Bible of Citeaux, 6, 41, 61
Bjerelsjoe, Sweden, 38
Blosius, 70
Boethius, 3, 20,
"Book of Customs," 5
Book of Lindisfarne, 60
bookbinding, 60-61
books, care of, 47-48
Boyle, Dom Bernard, 1
Boyle Abbey, 18, 28
Boyne River, 7
Brash, Richard Rolt, 34
Braun, Hugh, 26
British Library, 1, 55
British Museum, 55
Bissey, Dom due, 40
Burgundy, 3, 4, 12

C

Callixtus II, Pope, 5
Cantor, role of, 45-49
Cassiodorus, Flavius Magnus Aurelius, 1, 68, 69
Charlemagne, Emperor, 42, 65
Charter of Charity, 5
Chatillon, 3
Cherlieu Abbey, 42, 43
choir books, 47-48
Christmas, 46
Cistercian Abbey, Graiguenamanagh, 1
Cistercian Abbey, Middleton, 2

Cistercian Order
Cistercian use of acoustic jars, 29-40
  anonymity, 43
  architecture, 19-28
  in Ireland, 7-18
  manuscripts, 42, 51, 55, 59-78
  and music, 1-2, 20, 51-52, 79-84
  and St. Bernard, 3-6
Citeaux Abbey, 4-6, 21-23
  Great Bible of, 6, 69,
  illumination forbidden, 60
  music, 41-43, 45
  plan of, 22-23
Clairvaux Abbey, 6-7, 9, 18, 42
  daughter houses, 17
  death of Malachy, 17
  established, 5
  library catalogue, 19
  monastery as model, 12
  monks in Ireland, 16-17
  music, 43
Cluny Abbey, 3, 4
Codex 291, Black Friars, Vienna, 1, 14
Coelfrith, Abbot of Wearmouth and Jarrow, 65
Consuetudines, 5
Cormac, monk, 1, 55, 59, 75
  colophon of, 74-75
  sight reading of, 53
  sight singing, 56
Cormac's Psalter, 51, 55, 59

D
David, psalms of, 68, 71
David, son of Stephen the Harper, 72
De Psalmorum Usu, 66
Denford, Northamptonshire, 39
Dijon, 3-4, 6, 51
Divine Office, 5
Downpatrick, County Down, 28
Duiske Abbey, 72
Dunbrody Abbey, 32-53, 38, 40

E
earthquake, 28,
Easter, 46, 48
Eugenius, Pope, 17
Exordium Parvum, 5
Exposito St. Augustine Psalmis, 66-68
Extreme Unction, 49

F
Fairwell, Lichfield, 38
Finbar, Brother, 79
  sight reading, 53

florid organum, 54
Fontaines Chateau, 3, 5
Fontenay Abbey, 28
foot (measurement), 24
Fountains Abbey, 30-31, 34
France, 4, 17, 51
Frater, 25
Frederick, Archbishop of Cologne, 5
Fuller, Sarah, 42
funeral service, 49

G
Gaudry of Touillon, monk, 4, 5
General Chapters, 5
Geoffrey of Ainay, monk, 5
geology, 28
Gerard, monk, 3
Germany, 3, 17
Golden Rule, 24
Gothic architecture, 21
Gradule, 6
Great Bible of Citeaux, 6, 51, 69
Greece (Greek), 72
Greek Theatre, 35-36
Gregorian chant, 41, 55, 73
  theory, 43
  verbal music, 73
  word settings, 54
Gregory, Fr., 40
Gregory the Great, Pope St., 41
  Pope Gregory, 3
Grey Abbey, 28
Guido, Abbot of Citeaux, 6
  monk, 6
Guido (Guy), Abbot of Cherlieu, 43,
Guido of Arezzo, 53-54
Guido of Eu. see Guido of Cherlieu, 42
Guy of Cherlieu, 42

H
Hahn, Hanno, 24, 27
Hahnloser, 24
Harding, Stephen, 4-6, 51
  chant, 41
Charter of Charity, 5
Harperstown Castle, Taghmon, 72
Harpur family, 72
Holy Cross Abbey, 72
Honnecourt, Villard de, 22-24, 52
Howlett, David, 74, 76
Huby, Abbot of Fountains, 30
Hugh, Archbishop of Lyons, 4,
Hugh of St. Victor, 19
Hugh of Vitry, monk, 5

Hymnarium Collectaneum, 5

I
Ilbodus, monk, 6
Inch Abbey, 28
Inis Padraig, 17
Inishlounaght Abbey, 14, 18
Innocent II, Pope, 7
"Institutions" (Cassiodorus), 68
Italy, 17

J
Jarrow monastery, 65
Jerome, St. (Gallican version), 1, 60
Ms 36929, 51–62
Johannes Scotus Erigena, 19
John, monk, 4,
John the Deacon, 41,

K
Kerry, County, 2,
Kyrie Eleison, 2,

L
La Ferte Abbey, 5,
Laetald, monk, 4
le Roy, Ode, 30
Lectionarium, 5
Leeds Church, Maidstone, 39
Lent, 48
Letters 545 and 546, Codex 291 Vienna, 1, 7
Lexington, Stephen de, 29
Liber Sancti Marie de Valle Sancti Salvatoris, 1
Liber Usuum, 5
Liturgy of the Hours, 45
Logue, Fr. Peter, 40
Louth, County, 8, 11
Luppett, Devon, 39
Lux descendit, 55

M
MacMurrough, Dermot, King of Ireland, 16
McNamara, Rev. Professor Martin, 76
Magnificat, 46, 49
Mainistir na Corann, Middleton, 2
Malachy, St., Archbishop of Armagh, 6-7, 14-15, 17-18
  Bernard's letter to, 14-15, 17
  death of, 17–18
  founds Mellifont, 7, 14
Manuscript 36929, 2, 51-54, 59, 60, 63-64, 66-68, 74, 81-82
  colophon of Cormac, 52, 75
  contents of, 63, 78
  illumination, 61

palaeography, 59
sight reading of, 53, 79
Codex 291, Black Friars, Vienna, 1, 7, 14, 16
illumination, 60-61, 78
scriptorium, 59-60, 62
Mattock River, 9-11, 13
measurement, rule of, 24
Meath, County, 11
Meerseman, Rev. G.G., OP, 14
melismatic organum, 54
Mellifont Abbey, 1, 5-8
books, 45
and Clairvaux, 16–18, 21
land grant, 7-8
plan and architecture, 2, 22
siting of, 9-11
Metz Chronicle, 39
Metz Monastery, 29
Gregorian chant, 41, 55, 73, 81-82
Micrologus, 43
Migne, J.P., 66, 68
Mile of Monbard, monk, 5
Milley, monk, 17
mirrors, 70
modes, 52, 80
Molesme Abbey, 4
Monasterboice Abbey, 8
Monasternenagh Abbey, 14
Morimond Abbey, 5
Morson, Fr. John, 40
Mount Melleray, France, 40
Mount St. Bernard Abbey, Leicester, 40
Mount St. Joseph Abbey, Roscrea, 55
  music, 55
  harmonics, 21, 37
musical instruments, 35, 68, 72

N
Neckham, Alexander, 61
Neoplatonism, 21
neumes, 53
Nile River, 9
Nivard, monk, 3
Notre Dame, Paris, 54

O
O Connairche, Christian, 12
occursus, 54
O'Cearbhail, Donnchad, 7-8
Octaves, 46
Odo, Duke of Burgundy, 4
officers, tablet of, 47
O'Leary, 72
Opus Dei, 5

organum, 54
orthography, 62
Our Lady of Bethlehem Abbey, Portglenone, 55, 79

P
Pachomius, 9
palaeography, 59-62
Paschal II, Pope, 4
Pebook Monastery, 9
Pentecost, 46, 74
Peter, monk, 4
Peter, pilgrim, 4
Pithoy, Claude, 35
plain chant. see Gregorian chant
Pontigny Abbey, 5
Portugal, 17
Prefatio seu tractus de cantu, 42-43
psalmody,29
psalms, 41, 46, 60-61, 63-68, 69, 72-74
commentary of St. Augustine on, 64
"divisions of Cassiodorus," in Ms 39629, 69
Pusillus eram, 74
Psalterium, 5
Pythagoras, 20-21

R
Rathkeltair, 28
Ratios of the Consonances, 20
Raynald, Viscount of Beune, 4
Regula St. Benedicti, 5
Regule de arte musica, 42-43
Reinle, A., 24
resonators, 34, 37
Retractions De Trinitate De Musica De Verá religione, 19
Richard, Father, 55
Rievaulx Abbey, 17, 42
Robert, monk, of Clairvaux, architect, 7, 12, 16, 18-19. 21
Robert, monk, of Molesme, 4-5
Roche, Geoffrey de la, 5
Roche, Milo, Bishop of Leighlin, 72
Rosglas, Monasterevin, 56, 61, 72

S
St. Andrew's Abbey, 28
St. Bénigne, Abbey of, 3
St. Martial, Limoge, 54-55
St. Martin, Angers, 38
St. Martin's Abbey, Tours, 66
St. Mary's Church, Youghal, 32, 34, 38
St. Mary's Tower, Ipswich, 39
St. Peter's Church, Norwich, 38
St. Vorles, 3
Salve Regina, 2

scriptorium, 25, 59-62
Shelbourne Priory, 4
sight reading, 53, 79
Simpson, Otto von, 21
singing lessons, 46-47
solmization, 53
Song of Songs, The, 2, 41
Spain, 17
Stephen the Harper, 72
Sub-Cantor, role of, 45-47
Sweden, 17, 38
Sweeney, C., 42

T
Tabennisi Monastery, 9
Tescalin, Bernard, 3
theatre, 35-37
Theiry, William, 70
Tonale Santi Bernardi, 42
Troyes library, 6, 19, 51

U
Urban II, Pope, 5

V
Vauclair Monastery, 21
vellum, 60
Vitruvius, 36
Vivarium Monastery, 68

W
water power, 12
Wearmouth monastery, 65
Whalley Abbey, 40
Wigbold, Abbot of Aduard, 12
William, Abbot of Rievaulx, 42,
William of Conches, 19
Wilmart, Dom, 19

Y
York Cathedral, 65
Youghal, County Cork, 32, 34

References

Chapter 2.

1. A Father of the Abbey of Gethsemani, Kentucky of the Order of Cistercians of the Strict Observance, Compendium of the History of the Cistercian Order, 1944, p.45.

2. Op. cit., p.23.

3. Op. cit., p.24.

4. Op. cit., p.27.

5. Op. cit., p.37.

6. Op. cit., p.50.

7. Op. cit., p.56.

8. Op. cit., p.57.

9. Op. cit., p.59.

10. Op. cit., p.60.

Chapter 3.

11. A first order stream is a consequent stream.

12. A second order stream is a subsequent stream tributary to a consequent stream.

13. Braunfels, W. Monasteries of Western Europe: the architecture of the Orders. London, 1972, p.103.

14. Op. cit., p.81.

15. S. Bernardi Opera Vol. VIII. Epistolae. J. Le Clerq and H. Rochais (eds). Romae Editiones Cistercienses, 1977, p.282.

16. Epistola DXLVI. Epistola confraternitatis ad Dyermetium Hiberniae Regem Dermot II, King of Ireland, who in the year 1148 gave the monastery to the monks of the abbey of Mellifont to found there the monastery of Vallis Salutis; Recueil II 316, N10; Jan 114-115 ("Jan": L. Janauschek, Originum Cisterciensium 1, Vienna, 1877); G. Carville, "The Cistercian Settlement of Ireland (1142-1541)" in Studia Monastica, p.31. [I have referred to this letter in The Impact of the Cistercians on the Landscape of Ireland, K.B. Publications, 2002.]

17. Codex 70/291 contains about 150 different letters of various authors, H M ML PR No.8939. Amongst these are two of St. Bernard's first published in Sancti Bernardi Opera Omnia as Letters 545 and 546, edited by Dom Jean Le Clerq OSB and H. Rochias, Vol. VII, pp.513-514. I thank Right Rev. Dom Aengus Dunphy, Bethlehem Abbey, Portglenone and Rev. Alphonsus, Prior of Mellifont Abbey for help with these translations.

18. "these" – Bernard seems to allude to the Irish monks who spent some time at Clairvaux to be trained in the Cistercian way of life.

19. "those" – namely the monks of Clairvaux.

20. King, Archdale A. Cîteaux and her elder daughters. London, 1954, pp.231-132.

21. Milley 1708 engraved by C. Lucas.

22. Bernard of Clairvaux. The life and death of Saint Malachy the Irishman. Translated and annotated by Robert T. Meyer. Cistercian Publications, Kalamazoo, Michigan, 1978, Cistercian Fathers Series Number Ten, No.112, p.139.

Chapter 4.

23. Willmart, A. "L'Ancienne Bibliothèque de Clairvaux", Mémoires de la Société académique … de l'Aube (Lyons), LV, LVI (1916).
24. De Trinitate IV, 2:4 (PL, XLII, 889) cited by Simson, Otto von. The Gothic cathedral, London, 1956, p.40.
25. Op. cit., p.40.

26. "Omnes autem in hac dispositione symphonies musicas invnenemus", De arithmetica II, (PL, LXIII, 1158) cited by Simson, Otto von. The Gothic Cathedral, London 1956, p.33.

27. Grout, Donald Jay, Palisca, Claude V. A History of Western Music. WW Norton & Company, New York, London, 6th edition, 2001, p.7. Citing The Fundamentals of Music, trans with intro and notes by Calvin M. Bower (New Haven: Yale University Press, 1989), Book 1, Chapter 10, p.18.

28. "Omnes autem in hac dispositione symphonies musicas invnenemus", De arithmetica II, 49 (PL, LXIII, 1158) cited by Simson, Otto von. The Gothic cathedral, London, 1956, p.50.

29. Braunfels, W. Monasteries of Western Europe, London, 1972, pp.45-6.

30. Braun, H. English Abbeys, London, 1971, p.72.

Chapter 5.

31. New Grove dictionary of music and musicians, ed. Stanley Sadie, London, 1980, p.57.

32. Letters from Ireland 1228-1229, Stephen of Lexington. Trans. with an introduction by Barry W. O'Dwyer. Cistercian Fathers Series, Kalamazoo, 1982, item 76, p.167.

33. Fowler, James. On the so-called Acoustic Pottery at Fountain Abbey. Yorkshire Archaeological Society Journal, Vol. III, p.1.

34. Ibid., p.4.

35. Ibid., p.7.

36. Extract from the seventy-eighth annual report of the Commission of Public Works in Ireland 1909-10, p.10.

37. Ibid., p.10.

38. New Grove dictionary of music and musicians, ed. Stanley Sadie, London, 1980, p.55. and Fitzgerald. E. *On acoustic vases and other relics discovered in restorations lately made in the Church of St. Mary, Youghal.* Trans Kilkenny Arch Soc. May 1854 p.304.

39. Fowler, James. *On the so-called Acoustic Pottery at Fountain Abbey. Yorkshire* Archaeological Society Journal, Vol. III, p.6.

40. Fitzgerald. E. *New Grove Dictionary of Music and Musicians. Ed. Stanley Sadie.* London 1980, p.56.

41. Op. cit., p.56.

42. Op. cit., p.56.

43. Fitzgerald. E. *On Acoustic Vases and Other Relics Discovered in Restorations Lately Made in the Church of St. Mary.* Youghal. Trans Kilkenny Arch Soc. May 1854 p.305. and Ingrid D. Rowland, Thomas Noble Howe (eds.) *Vitruvius: Ten Books on Architecture.* Cambridge University Press, 1999, Chapter 5, pp.67-68.

44. The New Grove dictionary of music and musicians, Vol. 1, p.53.

45. The New Grove dictionary of music and musicians, Vol. 1, pp.54-55.

Chapter 7.

46. Regulations of the Order of Cistercians of the Strict Observance. General Chapter, Dublin, 1926, pp.285-286.

Chapter 8.

47. Hoppin, Richard H. Medieval music. The Norton introduction to music series, New York, 1978, pp.201-203.
    Illustration: page 57, Guidonian Hand, Wikipedia.

Chapter 9.

48. Cassiodorus, Catholic Encyclopedia.

Chapter 10.

49. Migne, J.P. Patroligiae Cursus Completus, Series Latina 1844-90, Paris.

50. Op. cit., pp.466-467.

Bibliography

Unpublished Sources

Ordinal of Rosglas. Rawlinson Manuscript Collection at the Bodleian Library, Oxford 1253-1753.

MS 36929 British Library, London.

Secondary Sources

Braun, Hugh. *English abbeys. London,* Faber & Faber, 1971.

Braunfels, Wolfgang. *Monasteries of Western Europe: the architecture of the Orders.* 2nd ed. London, Thames & Hudson, 1972.

Bucher, François. *Cistercian architectural purism.* Hague, Mouton, 1960-61.

Carville, Geraldine. *A Cistercian grange and the adventures of Captail Cuellar.* The Spanish Armada 1588, Bliainiris thir Chonaill, Donegal Annual No. 42, 1990.

Carville, Geraldine. *A historical-geographical and archaeological study of Cistercian Abbeys in Medieval Ireland.* Melanger de Dimier (ed.). Professor Cauvin, Dijon, France, 1981.

Carville, Geraldine. *A new look at old Mellifont.* Hallel, Vol. 28, No. 2, 2003. Roscrea.

Carville, Geraldine. *A town remembers.* Carlow, Nationalist Press, 1980.

Carville, Geraldine. *Abbey Assaroe, Abbey of the Morning Star.* Donegal Democrat, November 1988.

Carville, Geraldine. *Baltinglass – Abbey of the Three Rivers.* Leinster Leader Press, 1985.

Carville, Geraldine. *Beverages in Cistercian monasteries in Medieval Ireland.* Communications, Vol. 4, 1972, France.

Carville, Geraldine. *Birr: the monastic city, Brendan of the Watercress.* Bray, Co. Wicklow, Kestrel Press, 1997.

Carville, Geraldine. *Chorus Sancti Benedicti.* Co. Cork, Middleton Press, 1980, 28pp.

Carville, Geraldine. *Cistercian agricultural heritage.* Avonmore, Farmer's Journal, Vol. 7, No. 3, June 1980, Ireland.

Carville, Geraldine. *Cistercian fisheries in Medieval Ireland.* Citeaux Commentari Cistercienses, France, 1971.

Carville, Geraldine. *Cistercian geology and their Medieval quarries.* The Journal of the Mining Heritage Trust of Ireland, Vol. 2, 2002. Carville, Geraldine. *Cistercian mills in Medieval Ireland.* Citeaux Commentari Cistercienses, France, 1973.

Carville, Geraldine. *Cistercian settlement of Medieval Ireland.* Studia Monastica, Abadia de Montserrat, Spain, 1970.

Carville, Geraldine. *Cistercian sheep farming in Medieval Ireland.* Citeaux Commentari Cistercienses, France, 1971.

Carville, Geraldine. *Creggan, a Celtic Christian site: tangible links with St. Jarlath, 3rd Archbishop of Armagh.* 1996.

Carville, Geraldine. *Holy Cross Abbey* (Broadsheets). Veritas, Dublin.

Carville, Geraldine. *Liber Sancte Marie de Valle Sancti Salvatoris.* The Historical Committee, Graiguenamanagh, Co. Kilkenny, 2004.

Carville, Geraldine. *Mellifont, an abbey in a quarry.* The Journal of the Mining Heritage Trust of Ireland, Vol. 4, December 2004.

Carville, Geraldine. *Monasterevin: a parish and its people on the eve of the millennium. 1999.*

Carville, Geraldine. *Norman splendour, Duiske Abbey, Graignamanagh.* Belfast, Blackstaff, 1979.

Carville, Geraldine. *St Mary's Abbey, Graney: to live the apostolic life.* Hallel, Vol. 27, No. 1, 2002. Roscrea.

Carville, Geraldine. *The Cistercian nuns of Ballymore, Co. Westmeath.* Cistercian Publications, Kalamazoo, USA.

Carville, Geraldine. *The heritage of Holy Cross.* Belfast, Blackstaff, 1973.

Carville, Geraldine. *The iron mines of County Laois.* The Journal of the Mining Heritage Trust of Ireland, Vol. 1, 2001.

Carville, Geraldine. *The Medieval Cistercians and the Irish Sea link.* Volume in honour of Ed. Mikkers, France, 1981.

Carville, Geraldine. *The occupation of the Celtic sites by the Canons Regulars of St. Augustine and the Cistercians in Medieval Ireland.* Cistercian Studies Series 56, Kalamazoo, USA, 1982.

Carville, Geraldine. *The road from Camus to Moone – "advance a step each day" – an expression of Celtic monasticism.* Monastic Studies, Montreal, Canada, 1983.

Carville, Geraldine. *The Spanish monk's grave.* Bliainiris thir Chonaill, Donegal Annual No. 42, 1990.

Carville, Geraldine. *The urban property of the Cistercians in Medieval Ireland.* Studia Monastica, Abadia de Montserrat, Spain, 1970.

Carville, Geraldine. *Trees, St. Bernard and elected silence.* Hallel, 1990.

Cistercian General Chapter. *Regulations of the Order of Cistercians of the Strict Observance.* Dublin, MH Gill, 1926.

Fitzgerald, E. *On acoustic vases and other relics discovered in restorations lately made in the Church of St. Mary, Youghal.* Transactions of the Kilkenny Archaeological Society, May 1854.

Fowler, James. *On the so-called Acoustic Pottery at Fountains Abbey.* Yorkshire Archaeological Society Journal, Vol. 3, 1873.

Grout, Donald Jay and Palisca, Claude V. *A history of Western music.* 6th ed. New York, London, WW Norton, 2001.

Hoppin, Richard H. *Medieval music.* The Norton introduction to music history series, New York, London, WW Norton, 1978.

Howlett, David. *The polyphonic colophon to Cormac's Psalter.* Peritia 8, 1995, 81-91.

King, Archdale A. *Citeaux and her elder daughters.* London, Burns & Oates, 1954.

Letters from Ireland 1228-1229, Stephen of Lexington. Translated with an introduction by Barry W. O'Dwyer. Cistercian Fathers series, Kalamazoo, 1982.

Mahn, Jean Berthold. *L'orde cistercien et son gouvernement, des origines au milieu du Xllle siècle (1098-1265).* Paris, E. de Boccard, 1945.

Parkes, M.A., Carville, G., Kelly, G. and Dowds, S. *The sandstone mines of Mount Charles, Co. Donegal.* The Journal of the Mining Heritage Trust of Ireland, Vol. 1, 2001.

Philosophical Transactions Number 156. *An introductory essay to the doctrine of sounds containing some proposals for the improvements of acoustics as it was presented to the Dublin Society, November 12, 1683 by Narcissus, Lord Bishop of Ferns and Leighlin.*

Rowland, Ingrid D., Howe, Thomas Noble and Dewar, Michael (eds.) *Vitruvius: ten books on architecture.* New York, Cambridge University Press, 1999.

Sadie, Stanley (ed.) *New Grove dictionary of music and musicians.* 20 vols. London, Macmillan, 1980.

Seventy-Eighth Annual Report of the Commissioners of Public Works in Ireland, 1909-10.

Simson, Otto von. *The Gothic cathedral: origins of Gothic architecture and the medieval concept of order.* London, Routledge & K. Paul, 1956.

Sturman, Paul. *Advanced harmony, melody and composition.* Cambridge University Press, 1995.

Sturman, Paul. *Harmony, melody and composition.* Cambridge